"Can You Run Away from Sorrow?"

NEW ANTHROPOLOGIES OF EUROPE

Michael Herzfeld, Melissa L. Caldwell, and Deborah Reed-Danahay, *editors*

"Can You Run Away from Sorrow?"

Mothers Left Behind in 1990s Belgrade

Ivana Bajić-Hajduković

INDIANA UNIVERSITY PRESS

This book is a publication of

Indiana University Press
Office of Scholarly Publishing
Herman B Wells Library 350
1320 East 10th Street
Bloomington, Indiana 47405 USA

iupress.indiana.edu

© 2020 by Ivana Bajić-Hajduković

Manufactured in the United States of America

Library of Congress Cataloging-in-Publication Data

Names: Bajić-Hajduković, Ivana, author.
Title: "Can you run away from sorrow?" : mothers left behind in 1990s
   Belgrade / Ivana Bajić-Hajduković.
Description: Bloomington, Indiana : Indiana University Press, [2020] |
   Series: New anthropologies of Europe | Includes bibliographical
   references and index.
Identifiers: LCCN 2020000308 (print) | LCCN 2020000309 (ebook) | ISBN
   9780253050069 (paperback) | ISBN 9780253050045 (hardback) | ISBN
   9780253050052 (ebook)
Subjects: LCSH: Families—Serbia—Belgrade—History. |
   Mothers—Serbia—Belgrade—History. | Emigration and
   immigration—Serbia—History. | Serbia—History—1992-
Classification: LCC HQ658.6.Z9 B4533 2020 (print) | LCC HQ658.6.Z9
   (ebook) | DDC 306.85094971—dc23
LC record available at https://lccn.loc.gov/2020000308
LC ebook record available at https://lccn.loc.gov/2020000309

1 2 3 4 5   25 24 23 22 21 20

To my mother and father

CONTENTS

ACKNOWLEDGMENTS

THIS BOOK HAS BEEN IN THE MAKING FOR a very long time. It could not have been realized without unwavering trust and support from the editorial team at Indiana University Press and many colleagues, friends, and family. Above all, the mothers who shared their lives and experiences have made this book possible. Most of them are no longer living, but their voices need to be heard. This book is a tribute to these extraordinary "ordinary" women.

I am forever indebted to Michael Herzfeld for opening the door to the world of anthropology. A chance encounter with Herzfeld's ethnographies about Greece as a postgraduate in Modern Greek Studies inspired me to embark on this new academic journey. I was doing research in Athens in spring 2003 for an MPhil thesis in Greek literature when a colleague gave me several books about Greece, all by Herzfeld. Once I read those books, there was no going back to Greek literature. Ethnography was the only way ahead for me.

As a latecomer to anthropology, I faced a steep learning curve. Daniel Miller provided unwavering support and guidance during my transition to anthropology and material culture studies at University College London (UCL). I owe special thanks to my fellow students at UCL and Danny's Dinner Group for their peer support and stimulating discussions: Anna Pertierra, Dimitris Dalakoglou, Magda Craciun, Wallis Motta, Panarai Ostapirat, Miran Shin, Marjorie Murray, and Zuzana Burikova. A special thanks goes to Julie Botticello, a colleague and friend from UCL who read many versions of the manuscript over the years and selflessly helped with the shaping of this book. Words cannot express thanks enough to Lucia Neva, who encouraged me to keep writing and believed in this book even when I felt discouraged.

David R. Prince from Prince Research Consultants (PRC) was a most understanding employer who generously allowed me to take months off to conduct my fieldwork in Belgrade. Sarah McCarthy was instrumental in helping me find my way at UCL and at PRC. Darya Feuerstein-Posner, a colleague from PRC and a wonderful friend, has been a source of encouragement, inspiration, and laughter for the past fifteen years.

Martin Kohli from the European University Institute in Florence, Italy, and the 2009–10 Max Weber postdoctoral fellows helped tremendously with their comments about the project on remittances that features in this book.

Over the past five years, I have enjoyed continuous support in my academic work from Troy Gordon, director at Syracuse University in London, and Meghan Callahan, assistant director for teaching and learning. I am grateful to my students at Syracuse University in London who have inspired the writing of this book with their questions, comments, and optimism.

I thank Melissa Caldwell for encouraging me to revisit the manuscript after a long break while I looked after a young family. Jennika Baines has provided excellent advice, in particular with curating a personal voice in the manuscript. I am deeply grateful to the anonymous reviewers who have improved this book with their comments and constructive criticism.

During the making of this book, I have lost both parents and welcomed twins to this world. These life-changing events have greatly influenced the writing, not only by making this process significantly longer but by giving it more depth and a vantage point for understanding the phenomenon of mothers left behind. My dear mother, Ljiljana, was with me every step of the way, in life and spirit, teaching me the meaning of mothers' sacrifice and love. My father, Ranko, never missed a chance to inquire about the progress of the book or to impart unsolicited advice, which, along with his inimitable sense of humor, I have sorely missed. Throughout all this time, my husband, Darko, has been my anchor and, together with our children, an endless source of happiness and laughter.

Finally, this book would not have materialized without the people who shared their stories, their time, and their friendship in London and Belgrade. I cannot name these special people to protect their privacy. This book is dedicated to the memory of the mothers who sacrificed all they had during the crumbling of Yugoslavia so that their children could have a better future.

Sections of this book were previously published in Daniel Miller, ed., *Anthropology and the Individual: A Material Culture Perspective* (Oxford, UK: Berg, 2009), 115–30; *Genero—Časopis za feminističku teoriju i studije kulture* 14 (2010): 25–48; *Food and Foodways: Explorations in the History and Culture of Human Nourishment* 21, no. 1 (2013): 46–65; and *Contemporary Southeastern Europe* 1, no. 2 (2014): 61–79. I thank the editors of these publications for their permission to publish revised sections in this book.

"Can You Run Away from Sorrow?"

INTRODUCTION

IN MAY 1991, MY FAMILY AND I WENT on a short May Day holiday to Istria, Croatia. There we met our friends Muharem and Marija, university professors from Sarajevo in their early sixties at the time.[1] A few days later, when it was time to say goodbye, a shadow of worry fell over us. Fighting had already started in Croatia, and no one knew how it would end. To ease the tension and reassure everyone, Muharem jovially yet sincerely exclaimed that if worse came to worst, everyone was welcome in Sarajevo, as nothing could ever happen there. Sarajevo, in Muharem's words, was the safest and most tolerant city in Yugoslavia.[2] The chasm between personal experience and public discourse continued to widen in the following months and years. Marija and her daughter fled to Belgrade when the war in Bosnia-Herzegovina started, while Muharem stayed in Sarajevo to face the horror of the Sarajevo siege. The war tore their family apart, just as it did thousands of other families throughout Yugoslavia.

In late June 1991, Slovenia and Croatia declared independence, followed by a ten-day war between the Yugoslav People's Army (*Jugoslovenska Narodna Armija*) and the Slovenian Territorial Defense (*Teritorialna obramba Republike Slovenije*).[3] While the unraveling of Yugoslavia was well underway, September 1991 marked the start of another school year for my generation. Our teachers carried on with their work as if nothing had changed. Despite any worries they might have had, the teachers marched on with their lessons, trying to keep us eighth graders from noticing the conflict. The fighting continued while we memorized every detail about the Julian Alps and the Dinaric mountains: this was still our homeland, as our Dalmatian geography teacher working in a suburban New Belgrade primary school taught us in the fall of 1991.

The brutal reality, however, found a way of seeping into everyone's lives, including us children. Our teachers' determination failed to hide the almost palpable fear surrounding the horrific events as they unfolded. Children talked at school about conversations overheard at home. The most popular girl in our class told us about a presumed imminent bombing of Belgrade. Even without such politically savvy friends, we had seen a fair amount of uncensored footage of dead bodies on television, courtesy of Radio

Television Belgrade broadcasting news from the war front all day long.[4] The world as we had known it and learned about at school was falling apart in front of us, without anyone explaining what was going on or why.

Our generation started high school the following September, in 1992. While our classrooms were exploding with newly arrived refugee children, our older siblings, relatives, and friends were leaving the country at the same dizzying rate.[5] Three of my first cousins left Belgrade in the first half of the 1990s in pursuit of a better life, education, and career opportunities in North America. Another close friend moved with her family to New Zealand as highly skilled migrants. Several classmates who came as refugees moved back to Bosnia-Herzegovina after the war ended, while others emigrated overseas through refugee settlement programs. At the same time, many nonrefugee friends left Belgrade for the United States on college sports and academic scholarships in the mid-1990s. With the North Atlantic Treaty Organization (NATO) bombing in 1999, even more people left the country. Some returned after the end of the war, while others left for good. Endless lines of people waiting for visas outside foreign embassies, trying to escape to anywhere, became a regular sight in the 1990s.[6] At one point in the 1990s, graffiti appeared on a building in a central Belgrade street saying, "The last one to leave, switch the lights off."[7]

Belgrade in the 1990s was a crossroads for thousands of people leaving as economic migrants and draft dodgers, on the one hand, and those seeking refuge from the war, on the other. The call-up of reservists in the summer and fall of 1991 was a major push factor for young men's emigration from Serbia. An estimated two hundred thousand young men fled the country to avoid being sent to war. Gagnon notes that this may have been one of the biggest draft resistances in modern history. Between 85 and 90 percent of young men from Belgrade who were called up to fight refused to serve.[8] In addition to local men trying to evade the draft, many refugees who fled war zones in Croatia and Bosnia-Herzegovina and came to Belgrade seeking shelter were picked up by the police and sent to the front. One friend who escaped from Sarajevo when the war started spent months hiding in friends' homes in Belgrade. He dropped his Bosnian accent overnight so as not to attract the attention of Serbian police, who would have sent him back to Bosnia if they had caught him in the city.

Stories like these were told in half-whispers at times. One often heard of a friend or relative's departure only after he or she had left the country. These accounts would not be heard in the public discourse until much later.

In her 2016 novel *Ravnoteža* (Equilibrium), Svetlana Slapšak, a renowned classicist and author, describes the efforts to hide draft dodgers and help them escape Serbia in the 1990s.[9] Women—particularly older women—in Slapšak's novel held a crucial role in these operations. And while *Ravnoteža* is a work of fiction, it bears an uncanny resemblance to real-life stories presented in this book. More than twenty years after the war ended in 1995, the experiences of older women have begun to find their place in the public discourse. This book gives a voice to women who lived through the turmoil of 1990s Serbia and whose stories would otherwise disappear in the crevices of "his-story."[10]

In the mayhem that enveloped the region of the former Yugoslavia in the 1990s, women were pushed to the margins of society. Their voices were drowned in the noise of the ideologues' ethnonationalist rhetoric, war calls, and everyday struggles for survival. As the crisis deepened, they switched to autopilot and soldiered on, trying to save what they could—sending their adult sons to relatives abroad to protect them from war, making cakes out of nothing when ingredients were scarce, and mending and making do as their female ancestors had done during previous wars and crises.

This is not to deny the tremendous efforts of many feminist activists and women's organizations in Serbia at that time offering an alternative voice to the nationalistic, misogynistic, and paternalistic rhetoric that dominated the public discourse.[11] On the contrary, while leading political figures were mobilizing the nation, women were busy trying to plug up the sinking ship that carried their families. Unfortunately, women's outcries were drowned both publicly and privately in the deafening noise of the war machinery, collapsed socialist state, and economic meltdown.[12] While some may argue about the reasons behind feminist activists' failed attempts to join forces with each other, pointing fingers of blame, male voices indisputably still dominate the public arena in most parts of the world. As Cambridge classicist Mary Beard reminds us in her acclaimed manifesto about women and power, "women are still perceived as belonging outside power."[13] For women's voices to be heard in public, argues Beard, women in antiquity had to become men or give up their right to speak to men. Two thousand years later, the situation has not changed that much. This book is one small step in helping women's voices and experiences be heard and saved from historical oblivion.

The organic nature of my research process, explained in the next section, brought the mothers left behind during their children's exodus into focus, highlighting the poignancy and struggles of this invisible side of migration. The loss experienced by mothers left behind, their coping mechanisms, and their everyday practices are explored through the study of material culture.[14] The study of everyday practices and engagement with the material world reveals incredibly rich and at times surprising insight about the relationships between mothers left behind and their migrant children. The gifts from children that mothers hold on to, the food they send to their migrant children, and the everyday rituals performed around their homes tell us more about how ordinary women experienced the collapse of the country than any history book documenting the unraveling of Yugoslavia in the 1990s.

Paradigm Shift: From Migrants to Mothers Left Behind

Why center on mothers, one might ask, and not fathers or siblings? My original plan was to work with a group of migrants from Serbia who came to London in the 1990s and then move to Belgrade and work with their families to see how family relationships were affected by migration.[15] The nature of this research changed halfway through the project. Shortly before I was supposed to move to Belgrade for the second leg of fieldwork, I discovered that only three of my London research participants would agree to put me in touch with their families in Serbia. This prompted a search for parents whose children had left for other popular migration destinations in the 1990s, including North America and Europe.

Another surprise in my Belgrade fieldwork was a significant gender imbalance.[16] In most cases, wives outlived their spouses, so fewer husbands and fathers were available for research. The prevalence of mothers over fathers in my research sample corresponds with the official statistical data from that period. At the time of my research in 2006, there were significantly more women than men in Serbia, especially among the older age groups.[17] The average life expectancy in 2006 was 69.7 years for men and 75.0 for women. This gender bias gave my research a different perspective. Instead of studying parents' relationships with their migrant children, I shifted to mothers and their migrant children. And with the majority of the mothers in this research over the age of sixty, this evolved into a unique study about older women whose voices are generally not heard or recorded in Serbia, the Balkans, or elsewhere.

As for relationships between siblings, the everyday struggle for survival of those brothers and sisters left behind, paired with a sense of abandonment and sibling rivalry, often created a distance between nonmigrant and migrant siblings. Years after their brothers had fled the country because of the war, many of the nonmigrant siblings I talked to felt alienated. For them, being the sibling of a draft dodger in 1990s Serbia, rife with nationalistic rhetoric, was not easy. Writing about draft dodgers in 1990s Serbia, Sasha Milićević points out that negative attitudes about young men who escaped the war were openly expressed. Draft dodgers, in the view of her informants, were cowards hiding "under their mother's skirt" or leaving their homeland altogether; they were "faggots" and "scumbags," people who were best avoided, as they failed a test of manhood as well as Serbhood.[18]

Mothers were the ones who had enabled their children to evade conscription. They had facilitated contact with relatives abroad who in turn sent invitation letters for visas to adult children looking to escape the country. Mothers had scraped together whatever foreign currency they had stashed away for an emergency, borrowing from relatives and friends to help their sons and daughters buy a one-way ticket. They had not done this expecting to be able to follow them or that their migrant children would reciprocate in some way but to see them safe, away from the conflict and destruction. They had wanted their children to prosper and fulfill dreams they could never achieve in a country torn apart by war and a series of economic crises. Regardless of whether their children were draft dodgers who had not returned home in ten or more years, after everyone else had turned their backs on them, mothers persevered in their practices of keeping the love and memory of their migrant adult children alive. While these sacrifices can be interpreted as a prime example of "self-sacrificing micro-matriarchy," my book points to a vicarious aspect of mothers' sacrifice.[19] Mothers created meaning, purpose, and stability through the everyday sacrifices they made for their children. The precarious conditions of their lives in the tumultuous 1990s made these sacrifices stand out as almost superhuman, inexplicable to anyone but themselves.

Working with migrants in London was an entirely different experience from my fieldwork with mothers in Belgrade. My recent arrival as a postgraduate student in London positioned me as an outsider who did not share the struggles of 1990s migrants. It was not unusual for everything about me to be scrutinized, from my name and surname, family roots, accent, age, and gender to my position vis-à-vis Slobodan Milošević's politics and my experience and memories of Yugoslavia. Migrants from the 1990s had often resorted to creative ways of legalizing their stay in the United Kingdom. Thus my interest in them often aroused suspicion and prolonged the time it took to build trust. None of this was an issue during my Belgrade field-work.[20] Elderly mothers loved sharing stories of their children's departures and new lives abroad, even though these were often painful reminders of their loss. More than anyone else, the elderly mothers I spoke with in Belgrade gave a definitive shape to this research: they yearned to talk about their migrant children, to share the love and pain that they had lived with daily since their children's departure many years ago. This discrepancy between migrants' and parents' experiences of family relationships pushed the pendulum for me toward the mothers' side of the story, as opposed to the much more well-documented and extensively researched experiences of migrants.

From Socialist Yugoslavia to Post-Socialist Serbia

The fall of Yugoslavia in 1991 had a profound impact on everyone, regardless of age, social status, or wealth. For the generations born in the 1960s and 1970s, the collapse of their homeland was a cue—or an imperative—for emigration in a quest for a safer, better, and more stable life elsewhere. For the older generations, however, emigration was not an option: they had nowhere to go. They gave whatever savings they might have had to their children to help them leave the country. The parents stayed to face the onslaught of events in the 1990s, which they could neither have anticipated nor comprehended—not after fifty or so years of a relatively good life in Yugoslavia.

The bloody dissolution of Yugoslavia came as a shock, the first in a series of blows that followed in quick succession. Three months after the United Nations (UN) imposed sanctions against the Federal Republic of Yugoslavia (the federation of Serbia and Montenegro) in late May 1992, industrial production fell by 40 percent.[21] As a result of halted industrial production, a ban on international trade, and state robbery of citizens' private bank accounts, the republic experienced a complete economic meltdown.[22] At the end of 1992, the inflation rate in Serbia and Montenegro reached 19,810 percent. This trend continued in 1993 when Serbia set a record for one of the highest hyperinflation rates in history, reaching 313 million percent (the monthly inflation rate) in January 1994. Hyperinflation in Serbia lasted for twenty-five months between 1992 and 1994 and as such was the third longest period of hyperinflation in history.[23] Prices doubled on a daily—sometimes hourly—basis, and empty shops became a regular sight. The average monthly salary dropped from USD 450 in December 1990 to USD 80 two years later, hitting rock bottom with USD 3–6 in December 1993.[24]

As a consequence of the UN embargo, factories either closed or operated at minimum capacity. By the end of 1993, 1.3 million workers were on a paid leave of absence—not working but receiving nominal salaries—while 750,000 were unemployed.[25] In November 1995, following the signing of the peace agreement in Dayton, Ohio, the UN suspended the embargo against Serbia and Montenegro.[26] However, the UN sanctions were not fully lifted until 2001 after Milošević's extradition to the International Criminal Tribunal for the former Yugoslavia in The Hague. Staggering hyperinflation and the constant influx of refugees from Croatia and Bosnia-Herzegovina wiped away everything familiar, replacing citizens' daily lives with tremendous uncertainty and perpetual change. Despite the relief that accompanied the partly suspended UN sanctions in 1995, the chaos continued until the end of the decade. The second half of the 1990s was marked by mass protests against Milošević and his electoral theft in the local elections (1996–97) and protests against abolishing the autonomy of the University of Belgrade (1998). The following year, on the brink of the twenty-first century, Serbia and Montenegro endured the NATO bombing that began on March 24 and lasted until June 10, 1999. In October 2000, Milošević was toppled from power following his electoral defeat. These events form the backdrop for analyzing the impact of massive outward migration from Serbia in the 1990s on mothers left behind.

The Sound of Silence: Mothers Left Behind

When I first planned this project, communication was supposed to be its central theme. I wanted to learn if and how people stayed in touch with family members following emigration prompted by war and economic crisis. One of the characteristics of the post-1990 wave of migration from Serbia was that regular visits home were rarely possible for most because of the war and the UN sanctions that, among other things, suspended flights to and from Serbia.[27] At the same time, people in Serbia were hit by one of the worst economic crises since World War II. Internet use was still in its infancy, with computers prohibitively expensive for most citizens in 1990s Serbia.[28] I wanted to know how people circumvented these all but insurmountable obstacles to keep in touch with their migrant children. Moreover, I wondered how the war, embargo, economic crisis, and difficulties in obtaining travel visas had an impact on family relationships.

For those who could afford computers and an internet connection, emails and Skype did play an essential part in keeping in touch in the early 2000s. However, computers were a household luxury and a rarity. In 2006, about a quarter of households in Serbia had a computer, and only 7.3 percent had a broadband connection.[29] Beyond the limited availability and prohibitive cost, the use of computer-mediated communication also required elderly parents to master the use of software in a foreign language (English) and to keep abreast of technology developments to be able to stay connected to their children's lives abroad. This was very challenging for most mothers. In the ten years from 1990 to 2000, poverty levels had more than doubled in Serbia, rising from 14.1 percent to 36.5 percent. While poverty mainly affected the rural population in the early 1990s, hardship disproportionally hit urban-area residents from 1995 on. In the first half of 2000, more than a third of the population in Serbia lived on less than USD 30 per month, while 18.2 percent lived on less than USD 20 per month.[30]

This rapid impoverishment of the urban population in the 1990s and early 2000s severely limited consumption. Under such circumstances, it is no surprise, then, that mothers felt cut off from their migrant children. Phone calls abroad from Serbia were costly, and with no phone cards for international calls, telephoning migrant children was limited to emergencies. At best, depending on their income, mothers could afford to call their children once a month from a landline telephone. The cost of computers, internet connections, and phone calls in the 1990s put many mothers of migrant children in a situation not dissimilar to that of a hundred years ago when telephone calls were reserved for emergencies and people mainly relied on letters. Compounded with the rare visits of migrant children—either because of their migration status in their host country, their fear of being arrested in their home country for evading the military draft in the 1990s, or the absence of direct flights to and from Serbia as part of the UN embargo—mothers of migrant children frequently found themselves cut off from their children's lives. The aforementioned infamous graffiti from a central Belgrade street—"The last one to leave, switch the lights off"—never felt so palpable as when talking to mothers of migrant children. With a few exceptions of somewhat younger, healthier, and more affluent parents who had more contact with their migrant children online (mainly since the 2000s) and in person, the majority of mothers were profoundly affected by losing touch with their children and not being able to hear, see, or participate in their lives during the 1990s.

As the project unfolded, I learned that communication went far beyond a narrow focus on phone calls, letters, or—from the early 2000s on—computer-mediated communication. Food and gifts, including remittances—more meaningful even than phone calls, letters, emails, or Skype calls and messages—were tangible, sensory, and symbolically pregnant.[31] As such, they delivered a powerful message to their loved ones. Their materiality was a physical embodiment of connectedness. Phone calls and letters in the 1990s were supplemented by sending food, recipes, books, and magazines—anything that would remind migrant children about their relationships with family and tradition. Sending grandchildren a little pocket money carried special significance for elderly mothers. It was the ultimate sacrifice: in times when foreign currency was so precious, a gift of spending money was a sign of one's deepest devotion and love, a vicarious sacrifice through which elderly mothers forgot their own hardships for a little while so that their faraway grandchildren could have an ice cream cone in their new home country.

From the perspective of a mother-child relationship, it is unsurprising that mothers, even when in real material need, tilted the balance to their side of the relationship by sending gifts of food and money to their migrant children and their families. This effort goes beyond the local significance of the "self-sacrificing micro-matriarchy" to the center of the mother-child relationship. This is a profoundly unequal and unbalanced relationship. A shift in power would imply either the end of a relationship or a drastic change in a mother's role in it.

Class: From Methodological Problem to Analytical Tool

In both London and Belgrade, my informants insisted that they were not the research participants I was looking for—that they were not "typical Serbs." Most of my London informants were adamant that they were not representative of my research, suggesting that I go to a church instead to find these typical Serbs. Parents in Belgrade considered rural migration and rural population's practices to be typical of Serbia but not of themselves as *Beograđani* (Belgraders). These claims point to one essential fact: this is a study of an urban population, and it is by no means representative of all of Serbia or of all Serbians. This insistence that I would find typical Serbs in a church also highlights the process of self-essentializing: while people protested against outsiders' stereotypes of Serbs and their often negative portrayal in foreign media, they also used thes.e ideas to differentiate and define themselves in opposition to what they considered to be the true Serbs.[32]

I let both my London and Belgrade informants explain why they thought they were not representative—not because I believe there is such a thing as "true Serbs" but because this could potentially lead to useful insights about the politics of identity among Serbs. In both cases—migrants in London and parents in Belgrade—their emphasis on urbanity and practices that allegedly differentiated them from the true Serbs highlights the tensions between the seemingly opposed urban, atheist, pro-European elites and rural, Orthodox, true Serbs.[33] These binary oppositions are a result of fifty years of rapid industrialization of a previously mainly agrarian society, as well as the socialist championing of education and urbanization as symbols of progress and modernity. In reality, the extent of industrialization's efficiency is questionable compared with how presumably urban and rural Serbs tend to see it.[34] Nonetheless, these urban-rural categories were still in place during my fieldwork in the mid-2000s, and people used them to position themselves in the social landscape of a disorienting post-socialist reality in Serbia.

The "other"—true—Serbs were labeled as *seljaci* (peasants), a term that has been in use in both public and private discourse in Serbia for several decades. In late-twentieth- and early-twenty-first-century discourse, *peasant* has come to be considered a "polluting and dangerous" category—the Other that "pollutes" one's sense of culturedness and shared urban experience.[35] In the 1990s, *peasant* became an umbrella term for someone who supported nationalism, admired war criminals and gangsters, listened to turbo-folk music, and disregarded city manners (*gradski maniri*).[36] Writing about the "frontline peasants" in Belgrade and Zagreb and how white socks came to symbolize them in the 1990s, Stef Jansen points out that the key relevance of white socks discourses lay with the urbanites who formulate them and thereby construct their own subjectivity as cultured urban citizens.[37] Peasants, in other words, were constructed by and for the presumed urban middle class as their negative reflection in the mirror. One does not exist without the other.

While this image of the peasant who comes to town from the countryside was sympathetically portrayed in popular culture and jokes throughout the prewar decades, during the Yugoslav wars any positive meaning was lost.[38] All that was left was a hollow symbol that represented the antithesis of modernity. The term *peasant* painfully pointed out the fragility of the foremost project of Yugoslav socialism—the industrialization of an erstwhile agrarian society. In the 1866 census, around 90 percent of the Serbian population were peasants. Half a century later, in 1910, the figure had only marginally decreased to 84.2 percent. Not even Serbia's unification with Croatia and Slovenia in 1918 changed this predominately agrarian demographic; the 1931 census figure recorded that 76.6 percent of the population in the Kingdom of Serbs, Croats, and Slovenes were agriculturalists.[39]

Yugoslav socialism spearheaded urbanization, industrialization, and education accessible to all as clear signs of the modern, progressive society it had aspired to become. Throughout Eastern Europe, peasants represented one of the biggest challenges to socialist projects. The Yugoslav version of self-managing socialism was no exception. Peasants were a category ideologically incompatible with the idea of a classless socialist society, yet in 1961 they constituted 49.6 percent of the Yugoslav population.[40] One way to incorporate peasants into the presumed "classless" Yugoslav society was by creating a category of "peasant-workers" who were employed in factories but also carried on with agricultural work. Sociological research from the late 1980s shows that peasants remained outside the social structure of the Yugoslav system, indicating that the society's social structure was a closed one.[41] The fact that peasants were the least socially mobile in Yugoslavia led economist Branko Horvat to say that "one does not become a peasant, but remains one."[42] In other words, peasants were social pariahs in Yugoslav socialism, systematically marginalized. Right up until the end of Yugoslavia, peasants remained socialism's bone of contention. This dangerous Other—the socialist bogeyman—was perfectly positioned to be (ab)used by the new political leaders at the end of the 1980s. Despite the fact that—or perhaps because—the majority of Belgraders in the early 1990s hailed from the countryside, carrying the "polluting Other" in themselves, they wanted to distance themselves from this dangerous "peasant" categorization. Urbanites used the term *peasant* to assert their difference and cultural supremacy evidenced in their everyday engagement with the material world around them.

When the mothers left behind spoke about their migrant children and what they exchanged with them, it was often in relation to the presumed notion that they were not typical parents of migrant children in Serbia.

"Typical" parents of adult migrant children presumably received financial support in the form of remittances from their children, unlike my group of self-professed "atypical" parents who refused to claim help, even if (or when) they needed it. Expressing what they considered to be a popular belief at the time, my informants thought typical parents of migrants were parents of *gastarbajteri* (guest workers).[43] Jansen notes a similar correlation between peasants and *gastarbajteri*, arguing that urban discourses considered that peasants had ample money, transnational connections from their previous *gastarbajter* experience, and enjoyed conspicuous consumption.[44]

For parents left behind, their practices in relation to migrant (and non-migrant) children anchored them in the ever-changing socioeconomic landscape of 1990s Serbia. Money was an extreme case in point: to receive a gift that had significant material value was something they associated with the other kind of parents—those with *gastarbajter* children. But beyond remittances, people engaged in many other practices in their everyday activities that embodied their values, social aspirations, and class. Through these everyday activities, people were able to maintain a sense of internal order in the whirlwind of the 1990s.

"The Last One to Leave, Switch the Lights Off"

This book peers into the darkness of the 1990s and the lives of mothers left behind after the massive emigration wave during the last decade of the twentieth century. It bears witness to ordinary people's experiences in this particular period. The combination of the fall of Yugoslavia and the wars that followed, economic collapse and hyperinflation, and the UN sanctions give a distinctive character to the exodus of the 1990s, setting it apart from all other migration waves from Serbia before or since. For years no official statistics about emigration from Serbia were available, and until 2002 government statistics counted migrants, regardless of their length of stay abroad, as permanent residents in Serbia.[45] This was a win-win situation for whoever was in power at the time—from socialist Yugoslavia to Milošević's Serbia—because it masked the unemployment rate, increased cash flow through remittances, and helped preserve the political status quo. Emigration was a highly practical way of relieving pressure on those in power, as it disenfranchised hundreds of thousands of migrants whose votes could influence election results. The emigration wave of the 1990s was not only the outcome of a perfect storm of events but also a ruthless and efficient way of keeping dissenting voices muted and far from Serbia.

While emigration from Serbia has continued post-2000, its effect on families left behind has been much less dramatic compared to the 1990s. My research in 2005–06 included several families with adult children who had left in the early 2000s. Their experiences were significantly different from those with children who had emigrated in the early 1990s.[46] Most of the obstacles to keeping in touch with migrant children in the 1990s have disappeared in the 2000s: digital technologies have become more affordable and widespread, and people's mobility has become easier with the suspension of UN sanctions and the normalization of air traffic in Serbia. The strict visa regime for the majority of European countries was abolished in 2009. More importantly, in 2006, Serbia passed the Amnesty Law, dropping the legal persecution of army deserters and others who evaded the wartime draft in the 1990s.[47] The severe isolation experienced by mothers left behind in the 1990s has been eradicated in the post-2000 period.

However, this victory does not diminish the relevance of research into the lives of mothers left behind in the 1990s. This book stands as a testament to the consequences that a lethal combination of war, post-socialism, hyperinflation, and UN sanctions had on mothers left behind. It also highlights women's resilience and collective and individual coping mechanisms for dealing with trauma experienced with the collapse of socialism and their familiar world. When that world contracted even further with the emigration of their children, their sense of loss and disorientation increased. The necessity of preserving, clinging to, and creating something—anything—stable in one's universe became paramount for survival.

These mothers looked to the intimacy of home where they could create comfort and order, arranging their memories through relationships with objects. Homes were also sites of mourning for their migrant children, for the departed but not yet dead. The similarity with grieving lay in rituals devoted to migrant children whose physical absence allowed, as in death, for imagining and idealization to take place. In contrast, a nonmigrant child's everyday physical presence in the parent's life would make it impossible for a mother to idealize him or her that way. A migrant child or grandchild in a photo was not a real child but an idealized image of what that child meant to a parent. Homes, as this book shows, were sites where memories could be preserved, created, or sometimes deliberately destroyed.

The case of Belgrade mothers and their seemingly irrational behavior toward migrant children—from whom they often refused to accept money that would have alleviated acute needs, insisting, rather, that they should be giving the children money—is typical of downward social mobility. Due to the severe pauperization in the 1990s, generations of Yugoslav middle class people found themselves debased and struggling to hold on to old values in an attempt to restore a sense of normality in their lives during the chaos of the 1990s. This old middle class from Yugoslav times still clung relentlessly to its prior habits and beliefs. Some of these class values manifested in parents' relationship with their children. Social norms dictated that mothers were there to protect children and look after them long into adulthood—they did not expect their children to sustain them or materially support them. Remittances thus became a highly contested gift that created tension and humiliation, distorting the power relation between parents and children, often with profound consequences for this most basic of kinship relationships. Having said this, it is important to note that this is the case for emigration from urban places; comparative research with *gastarbajteri* originating from rural parts of Serbia supports the seemingly nonproblematic relationship between money and blood ties.[48] These differences in gifting practices and in valuing children between rural and urban Serbia indicate the coexistence of norms typical of preindustrial and industrial Serbia. This simultaneity of contradictory norms and values often caused friction between family members, as many of the examples in this book demonstrate.

Food was another gift that often provoked tension, frustration, and disappointment. Gift exchange between migrants and their parents, contrary to Marcel Mauss's argument, did not constitute that relationship through reciprocity.[49] Rather, gift exchanges established a claim to the categories of the persons involved. In other words, gift exchange serves to stipulate what it means to be a mother or a child. One gives food not to remember the food itself or because one expects to receive something in return; one gives food to remind the recipient of who she or he is to the giver. For example, when a mother sends a bottle of *šljivovica* (plum brandy) to her son in London, she does so not because he really likes to drink it but because it reminds him of who he is to his mother; similarly, a jar of *ajvar* (red pepper and eggplant spread) that an aunt sends from Montenegro to her niece in London is supposed to remind the niece of her place in her relationship to her aunt, as well as her place in her *familija* (extended family). The bottle and the jar are not there to be remembered for their contents but to make the recipients acknowledge much deeper memories—that of the way they were brought up and socialized into the world; of those who participated in their upbringing; and, implicitly, of their ancestry, their place of origin, and the kinship structure that they are still a part of regardless of how far away they may live and how long it has been since they last returned to visit. The role of gifting, in the case of migrants and their Belgrade mothers, is thus to persuade a recipient to acknowledge a memory she should already have of her own identity as an inalienable aspect of herself. This takes us further away from Mauss and closer to Annette Weiner and her discussion of the role of "inalienable possessions."[50] The gifts sent to migrant children and their families are not about what can be given away but about what can never be taken away—the inalienable nature of identity given in the relationship itself and one's position vis-à-vis parents, aunts, and relatives within one's *familija*. The loss of inalienable possessions, according to Weiner, "diminishes the self and by extension the group to which the person belongs."[51] What is contained in these inalienable possessions, in Weiner's view, is "the power of cosmological authentication," since they invest one with a power that transcends oneself and goes back to his or her ancestors. With the gradual passing away of those mothers whose children had left in the early 1990s and the consequent end of their relentless efforts to pass on the memory of families and ancestors to their migrant children, one wonders if the end result will be loss, as suggested by some of the mothers in this book. In other words, is the loss of the matriarch in Serbia also the loss of the 1990s migrants and everything and everyone they left behind?

Organization of the Book

Chapter 1 analyzes how people navigated food scarcity in the 1990s and sets the scene for the rest of the book. This chapter is based on fieldwork conducted from 2007 to 2014, a few years after the main fieldwork from 2005 to 2006 on which most of this book is based. For mothers whose children left the country in the 1990s, one of the most predominant memories was that of a constant struggle to conjure meals out of nothing. The hyperinflation of 1993–94 had emptied the grocery stores of foodstuffs, which were rationed or in short supply (except on the black market, which nonetheless required foreign currency to make purchases). Even the *pijace* (food markets) where farmers sold fresh produce were of little help: unlike people's salaries, their prices were tied to hard currency. Mothers whose children emigrated to nearby European countries in the early 1990s were in a different position, though not necessarily one that was less complicated. When their children tried to send food from abroad, parents struggled to accept such gifts. Mothers considered themselves to be feeders and providers, not recipients of food from their children.

The subject of food and foodways is further explored in the subsequent chapter. Food, as described in chapter 2, was very significant not only for post-1990 migrants but for the families they had left behind as well. While food from home elicited different memories—and sometimes conflicting feelings—for post-Yugoslav migrants, it helped many of them settle into their new countries and bridge the gap in their identity left by the dissolution of Yugoslavia. For many mothers left behind, food was one of the most powerful and significant channels of communication with their migrant children. In this chapter, we examine cooked food and recipes sent from one's home as well as processed foods from one's "home."[52]

Chapter 3 analyzes the material culture of home for parents left behind. By looking at everyday practices within homes, we see how people created meaning for their world through the physical objects and spaces there.[53] Homes are sites where memories are created and dwell. For parents, home is a living memory of their family, of the children they raised there, of meals they shared, of fights they had with each other—all the good and bad moments they spent together.

Stitched tapestries featured prominently in many homes that I visited. For numerous mothers whose children had left the country in the 1990s, weaving became a way of creating meaning and order in their lives. Photographs were another way of putting life in order—parents would furnish their apartment with countless photographs, often printed in black and white on plain paper and taped to the walls. People created routines around these objects, such as working on them (in the case of tapestries) at regular times of the day or walking past them in a particular way and at a specific time of day. This active engagement with things in the home allowed people to create still moments and restore a sense of order to counteract the disorienting world outside their walls.

The theme of sending contested gifts continues in chapter 4, which analyzes the phenomenon of remittances. At the time of my fieldwork, remittances regularly featured in Serbian public discourse, as they contributed more to the country's economy than foreign direct investments (FDIs).

Despite this, neither the migrants in London nor the parents in Belgrade whom I spoke with seemed to have any significant involvement in the practice of sending and receiving money on a regular basis. Remittances are deeply embedded in the social fabric of Serbian society, however. They are not a post-socialist phenomenon but one that goes back to the days of Yugoslav *gastarbajteri* in Germany from the 1960s on. Strict norms embedded in social relations dictated how money received from abroad should be distributed in one's home country.

The everyday practices of migrants and parents included engagement with various means of communication to keep in touch with each other. Meticulous letter writing was not only a way of passing on one's thoughts and feelings; writing in cursive Cyrillic was a mother's attempt to preserve her son's knowledge of the language and provide a conscious reminder of his origins. Chapter 5 closely examines communication practices—what they entailed and why. As with most of the everyday practices, these had quite a different meaning for parents than for their migrant children. While parents were more involved in the transmission of knowledge, norms, and attempts to keep their children knitted into the social fabric of their lives through communication, children were more interested in sharing their experiences, achievements, and problems in their destination countries.

The consequences of migration on family relationships, particularly those between mothers and children, are analyzed in chapter 6. Migration had different effects on families and family members over time. Despite the strong normative character of family relationships in Serbia, the 1990s wave of emigration transformed people's experiences of family in a more experiential direction. Family appeared not as "a naturally occurring collection of individuals" but was instead made through daily activities and interactions (like eating) performed together.[54] The 1990s wave of migration reshaped not only people's relationships with families back home but their own subjectivity as well. Motherhood and death had transformational effects on people. Becoming mothers or losing family members shifted a paradigm for many migrants. Such events created a seismic shift in migrants' sense of subjectivity. This is analyzed in chapter 6 as well, which explores the impact of these life-changing events on one's relationship with oneself and with one's family.

Each chapter consists of several portraits chosen as representative of the particular topic. Some portraits are included because they stand out and offer a contrasting perspective that complements the so-called typical cases. Others have been chosen for their richness, which allows us to analyze more complex issues without removing the poignancy and intimacy of ethnographic encounters. The book deliberately focuses more on the narratives of mothers left behind than on presenting their migrant children equally alongside them. This was a conscious decision not only because of the uniqueness of the experiences of those left behind in general but because of the specific period, the 1990s in Serbia: the time before webcams, smartphones, and free apps for messages and calls; the time before cheap flights—or any flights—to and from Serbia; the time of endless lines outside embassies in Belgrade for visas to almost any country in the world; the time of complete isolation that affected everyone but particularly hit elderly parents whose children had left in search of safety, stability, and opportunities. This is not to say that migrants' experiences in London were all positive or easy ones; far from it. But they had hope. Sometimes it took them five or ten or more years to settle down, regulate their immigration status, get a degree or build a career, get a mortgage or start a family, but they all did so eventually. During that period, their elderly mothers and fathers bore the brunt of socioeconomic changes that brought them poverty, humiliation, loss of dignity, illness, and, eventually, the end of life instead of hope for something better to come. Their experience is incommensurable with that of migrant children and deserves to be placed in the spotlight. This explains the limited presence and relative silence of migrants in this book.

The massive scale of emigration from Serbia in the 1990s created a fracture in mothers' identities, as we see in the stories in this book. While hundreds of texts and studies have documented this sense of rupture in migrants' identities, we still know very little about the effect of migration on those who stay behind.[55] For years, mothers left behind had suffered in silence; no one wanted to know about their pain. Trapped between the envy fueled by stories about the billions of dollars that migrants were sending to their families, on the one hand, and the public condemnation of draft dodgers on the other, mothers left behind were sentenced to silence. Although the war that propelled this migration wave has long since ended, several other wars around the world have in the meantime forced millions of migrants to flee their homes. Long columns of migrants hide the invisible other side of migration: that of elderly mothers left behind. Their trauma and suffering is no less than that of migrants trekking toward safety and a better life. It is time to break this silence and give women the voice and space to share their experiences.

Notes

1. All the names in this book are pseudonyms to protect people's privacy. I have used first names only, keeping them in the original Serbo-Croatian transcription. Public figures, which are cited by full name, are the only exception.

2. Throughout this book, "Yugoslavia" refers to the Socialist Federal Republic of Yugoslavia (SFRY), a country that existed from 1946 to 1992. Serbia and Montenegro formed a federation in 1992, the Federal Republic of Yugoslavia, that existed until 2003. From 2003 to 2006, Serbia and Montenegro formed the State Union of Serbia and Montenegro. Following Montenegro's exit from the union in June 2006, Serbia and Montenegro became independent countries.

3. See Silber and Little, *Yugoslavia*; Ramet, *The Three Yugoslavias*; Cohen and Dragović-Soso, *State Collapse*; Gow and Carmichael, *Slovenia and the Slovenes*; and Alcock, Milivojević, and Horton, *Conflict in the Former Yugoslavia*.

4. In his book *The Myth of Ethnic War: Serbia and Croatia in the 1990s*, Chip Gagnon describes how "official Serbian television bombarded its viewers with these visuals in 1991 with accompanying discourse to highlight the horrors" (2). Gagnon does not mention here that this footage was broadcast throughout the entire day, without any warnings about the scenes that followed, thus exposing children to these horrific images and discourse.

5. At the start of high school in 1992, my grade had six classes, each with around thirty children. Halfway through high school, in 1994, we had seven classes with more than forty students in each class. This increase in the number of children reflected an influx of refugee children arriving from Croatia and Bosnia. Some children arrived unaccompanied and lived in a care home for high school students, whereas others lived with relatives.

6. Dejan Cukić, a famous pop-rock singer from Belgrade, recorded a song in 1998 entitled "Zimbabwe," calling on people to move there. The song reflected reality, with Zimbabwe and South Africa being popular migrant destinations in the 1990s. Any destination out of Serbia was a popular one back then—people were flocking to anywhere and everywhere around the globe in the 1990s.

7. *Ko poslednji izađe, nek' ugasi svetlo.*

8. Figures are from Vesna Pešić, Centar za Antiratnu akciju [Center for Antiwar action], Belgrade, cited in Gagnon, *Myth of Ethnic War*, 2.

9. Slapšak, *Ravnoteža* [Equilibrium].

10. Hundreds of titles document the Yugoslav wars in the 1990s. For a summary of this literature, see Baker, *The Yugoslav Wars of the 1990s*.

11. See, for example, Blagojević, "Biti Srbin, biti muško" [Being Serbian, being a man]; Hughes, Mlađenović, and Mršević, "Feminist Resistance in Serbia"; and Papić, "Women in Serbia."

12. For more details about the feminist organizations in 1990s Serbia, see Blagojević, *Ka vidljivoj ženskoj istoriji* [Toward a visible female history].

13. Beard, *Women and Power*, 56.

14. My formal training in anthropology at University College London was anchored in material culture studies and informed by research in this field conducted by Daniel Miller, Michael Rowlands, Victor Buchli, and others. This approach is heavily indebted to Pierre Bourdieu's work laid out in *Outline of a Theory of Practice*.

15. The ethnographic project took place in London and Belgrade in 2005 and 2006, followed by several subsequent research visits to Belgrade from 2006 to 2014.

16. Within the parents' group, twenty-seven were female and only six male.

17. In the 65–69 age group, there were 120 women for 100 men, whereas in the 75–80 age group, this ratio was 166 to 100. (*Žene i muškarci u Srbiji* [Women and men in Serbia].)

18. Milićević, "Joining the War," 281.

19. Marina Blagojević Hughson, a feminist activist and sociologist, coined the term "self-sacrificing micro-matriarchy" to describe the tremendous sacrifices women in 1990s Serbia made for their families. While Blagojević did not write specifically about mothers of migrant children, I find her research framework particularly fitting here. For more on "self-sacrificing micro-matriarchy," see Blagojević, "War and Everyday Life."

20. All my informants in Belgrade lived in apartment buildings, and a large number were based in New Belgrade (Novi Beograd). New Belgrade was built after World War II as a bedroom suburb for blue- and white-collar workers.

21. Stamenković and Pošarac, *Makroekonomska stabilizacija* [Macroeconomic stabilization], 21.

22. Dinkić, *Ekonomija destrukcije* [The Economy of destruction].

23. Hanke and Krus, "World Hyperinflations," 12.

24. Antonić, *Zarobljena zemlja* [Arrested country], 112, 162.

25. Stamenković and Pošarac, *Makroekonomska stabilizacija*, 29.

26. Delević, "Economic Sanctions."

27. After several decades of visa-free travel to and from Yugoslavia, most countries, including the United Kingdom, introduced a visa regime for Serbian citizens in November 1991. The UK visa regime was still in place in early 2020, even though the visa requirement for the Schengen Area in the European Union (EU) was abolished in 2009. To apply for a tourist visa to visit a family member in the United Kingdom, one needed an invitation letter from a migrant son or daughter who had to document his or her right to stay in the United Kingdom (either permanent residency or a British passport) and provide bank statements for the last six months as proof of financial means to support the parents during their visit. Parents wishing to visit their children also had to prove they had sufficient financial means to support themselves during their stay and were required to include not only their pension statements but also savings account statements and proof of property ownership—all translated into English. These requirements made it virtually impossible for the majority of parents in the 1990s to visit their migrant children in the United Kingdom. Travel from Serbia to the United Kingdom was further complicated in the 1990s by nonexistent flights as a consequence of the UN embargo. One had to take a bus from Belgrade to Budapest or Vienna and from there catch a plane for the United Kingdom, making this journey even more difficult for elderly passengers.

28. This was the time of slow and costly dial-up internet connections. Desktop computers in mid-1990s Serbia cost between USD 900 and 1,200, whereas an average monthly salary was around USD 100. In effect, this put computers and the internet out of reach for most Serbian citizens during the 1990s.

29. Kovačević, Pavlović, and Šutić *Upotreba informaciono-komunikacionih tehnologija* [The use of information and communication technologies], 13–17.

30. Bogićević, Krstić, and Mijatović, *Siromaštvo u Srbiji* [Poverty in Serbia], 36–37.

31. The term "remittances" in this book defines personal financial transfers from abroad to families in Serbia. They can be made via bank, money transfer operators, or in person.

32. "Church Serbs" were a mix of Serbs from different immigration waves and various parts of the former Yugoslavia—mostly the first generation of anticommunists and

their descendants and a mix of post-1990 ethnic Serbs from Serbia, Croatia, and Bosnia-Herzegovina. For an excellent discourse analysis of the politics of identity among Serbs, see Čolović, *The Politics of Symbol*.

33. The urban-rural division in Serbian discourse is the subject of extensive academic research; see, for example, Rihtman-Auguštin, *Ulice moga grada* [The streets in my town]; Vujović, *Grad u senci rata* [A city in the shadow of the war], 71–105; Brown, "Beyond Ethnicity"; Čolović, *The Politics of Symbol*; Jansen, *Antinacionalizam* [Antinationalism]; Jansen, "Who's Afraid of White Socks?; and Spasić, "ASFALT"[Asphalt].

34. For a discussion of the rural-urban paradox, see Simić, *The Peasant Urbanites*, and Matić, "Urban Economies."

35. Douglas, *Purity and Danger*.

36. The city manners loosely referred to unwritten rules for behavior in urban places, such as not throwing rubbish on the streets, not spitting, not being too loud in public, holding a door for the next person, being courteous, being respectful toward public spaces, not destroying public gardens or benches, etc.

37. Jansen, "Who's Afraid?"

38. Patterson, *Bought and Sold*.

39. Šljukić and Šljukić, *Zemlja i ljudi* [The land and the people], 60.

40. Ibid., 99.

41. Popović and Bogdanović, *Društvene nejednakosti* [Social inequalities], 331–40, cited in Šljukić and Šljukić, *Zemlja i ljudi* [The land and the people], 126.

42. Horvat, Ogled o jugoslavenskom društvu [An essay about the Yugoslav society], quoted in Šljukić and Šljukić, *Zemlja i ljudi* [The land and the people], 126.

43. *Gastarbajter* is a Serbo-Croatian rendition of the German word *Gastarbeiter*, meaning "guest worker." With time, *gastarbajter* has come to denote a guest worker from Yugoslavia living anywhere in the world. Thus, people in Serbia nowadays speak of *gastarbajteri* in America, Canada, Australia, and so on.

44. Jansen (2005b), "Who's Afraid?," 163.

45. Stanković, *Popis stanovništva* [Census of population], 98.

46. During my research in 2006, already there were some Belgrade families who regularly kept in touch with their migrant children through Skype and email; this made a big difference to their experience of proximity and family intimacy. It is worth noting that parents whose children left after 2000 were younger, financially better off, and healthier than those whose children left in the early 1990s, and could more easily visit their children abroad.

47. Zakon o amnestiji [The Amnesty Law].

48. Stanković, *Popis stanovništva* [Census of population], 96–98; Petree and Baruah, *A Study of Migrant-Sending Households*.

49. Mauss, *The Gift*. According to Mauss, gift giving creates an obligation to repay within a specific time frame. The gift, thus, establishes a relationship between a giver and a recipient through an obligation to repay.

50. Weiner, *Inalienable Possessions*.

51. Ibid., 6.

52. I deliberately put this term in quotation marks because "home" in this case is different from one's parents' home and stands instead for the migrants' country of origin—Yugoslavia.

53. This focus on people's engagement with their material world is embedded in the work of Pierre Bourdieu. See Bourdieu, *Outline of a Theory of Practice*.

54. DeVault, *Feeding the Family*, 39.
55. A few exceptions include studies about Filipina migrant workers and their children: Parreñas, *Children of Global Migration*, and Miller and Madianou, *Migration and New Media*. However, both studies focus on children left behind and their relationships with migrant mothers. Elderly parents left behind are the subject of an excellent study by King and Vullnetari, "Orphan Pensioners and Migrating Grandparents."

1

THE LOCUST YEARS

"THESE ARE THE YEARS EATEN BY LOCUSTS," I heard my mother say with a noticeable hint of despair in 1993. The exact meaning of her words was lost on me at the time.[1] I had not lived through the "locust years" discussed in the memoirs of two distinguished men writing about the buildup to World War II (Winston Churchill) and its aftermath (Borislav Pekić) and was too young to understand the very personal meaning these words had for a fifty-something-year-old woman struggling with an ever-changing reality in Serbia in the 1990s.[2] Unlike the promised restoration that followed the "locust years" in the Bible, neither victory nor redemption awaited women of the former Yugoslavia after the 1990s. They suffered loss after loss after loss. The locust years gnawed at their families, their financial independence, and their health, faith, and dignity. None of these losses were restored to them, despite their extraordinary efforts to keep their households and families afloat. These ordinary women may slide down the vortex of history, silent and invisible, as have so many women caught up in conflict and hostilities before them, if they are not given a voice.

Just as World War II affected those on the home front, the political and economic crises in the 1990s transformed daily reality for everyone in the former Yugoslavia. From the most visible changes in how people traveled to work or school or formed lines to secure food in eerily empty markets to the more invisible changes in the intimacy of one's home with increasingly empty refrigerators and dinner plates, the transformation of the material world was ubiquitous. Before the Yugoslav wars, an average of 1,500 buses transported approximately 1.5 million Belgraders across the city every day. In 1994, only a third of the buses were left on the roads because gasoline was so scarce. People still moved around the city somehow, usually hanging from buses because the doors, bulging with crammed bodies, could not close.

Waiting for the next bus in the 1990s did not necessarily guarantee a seat because the next bus would arrive already bursting with passengers jammed between the doors. The longer one waited, the more people would arrive at a bus stop, angry, desperate, and ready to break their own or anyone else's back just to board the next bus because they had to get to the office, school, or hospital. But these were not ordinary times. These were the locust years.

This chapter explores the turmoil in Serbia during the 1990s and how people coped with the scarcity of food during this period of crisis. While some post-Yugoslav migrants, particularly those who left during the hyperinflation period in 1993, were aware of the conditions in the country, others had no idea of the actual scale of the crisis or their families' experiences. Mothers, wanting to protect their migrant children from knowledge of the brutality of their everyday lives, put on a brave face for them. In reality, the 1990s were a traumatic experience for the majority. When I asked people ten, even fifteen years later to share their memories from the early 1990s—how they got by and fed their families—a few women turned down my request, saying they did not and could not remember this period. Even when I asked to look at their handwritten cookbooks and recipes from that period, they told me they could not find them. Some women openly admitted it was too disturbing to revisit the recipes from that period. Their experience of "ordinary life" was so abnormal in the 1990s that they had deliberately erased it from memory. Not everyone, however, wished to forget the severity of the 1990s; their memories and recipes provide a backdrop for understanding the scale of sacrifice borne by women in their everyday struggle for their family's survival.

Bread and Lard Revisited

With the economic crisis in the 1990s, consumption patterns changed dramatically. People adapted their diets to their rapidly crumbling world. Old methods of preparing food, as well as recipes with fewer and cheaper ingredients, found their way back into Serbian kitchens. Instead of cooking with expensive sunflower oil, women turned to a staple of their mothers and grandmothers. Lard, a by-product of pig rearing, was readily available in the countryside, and many city dwellers relied on their rural relatives for help with providing food, including lard.

The interconnectedness between the city and the country has been a safety valve during various crises since the end of World War II, despite the socialist regime's attempts to dismantle the peasant society in Serbia.

In the postwar years, rapid industrialization and urbanization transformed the Serbian peasantry. Yet many of the cultural traits and traditional norms typically found in the peasant society have survived the peasants' move to the cities. American anthropologist Andrei Simić studied the effects of rapid urbanization in Serbia more than forty years ago.[3] "Peasant urbanites" whom Simić observed in early 1970s Serbia brought their traditions from the countryside to the urban settings. The crisis in the 1990s reaffirmed Simić's findings, attesting to the resilience of peasant culture in urban settings.

Croatian author Pavao Pavličić humorously writes in his book *Kruh i mast* (Bread and lard) about his father, who said that he had eaten so much bread and dripping in his lifetime that the slices would reach the sky if placed one on top of another.[4] Later on, Pavličić writes, they switched to margarine, then butter, until they stopped using any form of spread and nibbled on bread alongside salami and cheese. In the end, they stopped eating bread because it was allegedly fattening, even though Paviličić and his father were "thin as pike" when they ate bread and lard.[5] Many of my informants gave similar accounts during my research, questioning, with a dose of nostalgia, whether health professionals were right after all in their claims that sunflower oil and margarine are healthier than lard. While the production and distribution of sunflower oil were state-regulated in Yugoslavia, lard was largely produced independently. Whoever reared pigs, or even just bought half a pig—often through a company union—got lard as a by-product of a head-to-tail approach to butchering. Unlike sunflower oil, which was susceptible to state-induced shortages, lard had a more stable presence in the market because its production was not state-controlled. However, the use of lard decreased in the 1970s and 1980s. Recipes calling for sunflower oil and butter gained in popularity, possibly because of health practitioners' claims against lard.

Lard's comeback in the early 1990s suggests that people relied on the knowledge from a preindustrialized peasant society to surmount the challenges that sanctions imposed on their usual diets. This shift from oil to lard consumption in the early 1990s was not only a sign of economic crisis but also resembled a journey through time, going back half a century to the period of food scarcity during World War II and subsequent rationing. Lard was used not just for cooking but also as a spread on bread—*mast i hleb*, the equivalent of bread and dripping in the United Kingdom. *Mast i hleb* was a well-known staple among the generations who grew up in the 1940s and 1950s without the butter, margarine, or cheese spreads that later became common. Postwar generations vividly remembered a childhood staple: a slice of bread topped with a thick layer of lard and sprinkled with salt and paprika.

Half a century later, *mast i hleb* once again became a favorite breakfast for many. Several of my female informants recalled having breakfast with colleagues at work during hyperinflation, a meal consisting of bread, lard, and yogurt. The difference this time was that everything was homemade, including the bread, because its stock was heavily limited in shops. Women who began baking bread at home in the early 1990s did not do so through choice or for a love of baking but because flour was about the only thing available.

One of my informants, Lola, a retired landscape architect, recalled: "We had a 50-kilo sack of flour in the pantry, and I baked three times a day, as there was hardly anything else to eat: bread for breakfast, pies for lunch, and buns for dinner, day after day, month after month. In the first six months after the end of hyperinflation, I refused to turn on the oven—I was so fed up with baking."[6] This phenomenon should not be compared to the revival of home baking in the West, where traditional methods of cooking and baking have regained popularity over the last two decades.[7] Even though a sense of nostalgia was present in people's recollections of the days of bread and lard, the memories were not fond ones. This food served as a sensory trigger for recollections of other, more difficult times. "Memory," Nadia Seremetakis writes, "is a culturally mediated material practice that is activated by embodied acts and semantically dense objects."[8] In other words, the revival of bread and lard in 1990s Serbia not only brought back memories from World War II, but people relived these memories through another period of hardship. This physical reembodiment of one's memories of life under duress may have sated a nostalgia for one's childhood, but it also triggered a stream of memories of war, hardship, and poverty. Bread and lard reappeared on plates not because of nostalgia or a food fad but because of necessity.[9] As soon as the economic situation improved, the consumption of lard went back to precrisis levels, stored away—physically and mentally—for future hardship.

Back to the Future: The Return of War Cookbooks

In the previous section, I point out the importance of foodstuffs from earlier periods of hardship, such as World War II and the years immediately after the war. The forced retraditionalization in cooking and baking in Serbia in the 1990s relied heavily on intergenerational transmission of knowledge gained during the war years. Interestingly, war cookbooks were produced during both world wars. One was even published internally for the needs of the Yugoslav People's Army in 1983.[10] The 1990s, however, had no such official cookbook, and the war cookbooks that people referred to in my interviews existed mostly in the form of recipes and knowledge passed on from previous wars and through informal channels.

As Jovanka, a university professor, noted: "Each generation here has a *ratni kuvar* [war cookbook] to which women resort in times of crisis. In difficult times, women start to recall their mothers, aunts, and grandmothers, what they cooked and baked during the war—for example, how to make jam without sugar, bread without yeast, apple cider vinegar, et cetera. I called these 'pauper recipes' rather than 'war recipes.' It wasn't tragic; we didn't starve during the embargo; it was often funny and amusing [how we got by]."[11]

Jovanka's perspective highlights two essential issues: transmission of knowledge and a derisive attitude to hyperinflation. The first was instrumental in coping with food scarcity because, in the absence of guidance from health (or any other) authorities, people relied on knowledge passed down through previous generations. The concept of "knowledge," in Fredrik Barth's view, "situates its items in a particular and unequivocal way relative to events, actions and social relationships."[12] Serbians' knowledge about methods of surviving food shortages and scarcity—for example, in the form of recipes in personal war cookbooks—was reproduced within particular groups or social networks. Jovanka explained that a friend and colleague who shared cost-saving recipes with her during the economic crisis in the 1990s had come across them in a war cookbook she had inherited from her mother-in-law, who, in turn, had compiled the recipes during World War II. Jovanka's friend's mother-in-law hailed from an established and well-off Belgrade family. Knowledge, as this case shows, is transmitted from one generation to the next, but furthermore, because it is embedded in social relationships, it reproduces values inherent to a particular class.

The other important aspect conveyed by Jovanka is an ironic attitude toward the hardship of the 1990s. People recounted hilarious situations from the hyperinflation period, such as waking up and stepping on a sack of flour next to one's bed. My informants did not complain of hunger in the 1990s but reiterated that flour saved everyone.[13] However, to feed a family mainly on flour, one had to become a dedicated baker with abundant creativity and the ability to adapt quickly to continuously changing circumstances in the food market, such as finding alternatives to leavening agents.

Lola showed me her handwritten cookbook from the early 1990s, which included a recipe called *Kolač od ništa* (cake out of nothing) that she had acquired from her brother-in-law. The recipe, of course, required several ingredients, contrary to what its name suggested. The underlying irony of this cake's name and the names of many other recipes from this period points to a derisive attitude toward the situation: Embargo Cake, UNPROFOR Cake, Crazy Dough (also known as Wonder Dough), Cake without Eggs, Rolls without Eggs, Madjarica (also known as The War Cake), and Embargo Schnitzel were some of the old-turned-new-again recipes that became part of an everyday diet during the embargo.[14] The names given to these recipes are suggestive. Even though there was no war front in Serbia (at least not in the first half of the 1990s), people who fled the war zones in Croatia and Bosnia-Herzegovina brought with them recipes that referred to the war (UNPROFOR Cake, The War Cake), thus the proximity of the war front blurred the lines of foodways, commingling recipes from the actual war zone with those from the embargo-induced crisis zone in Serbia.

These recipes contained two common elements: a few essential ingredients combined with improvisation and creativity. For example, fruit could be substituted with jam, or vice versa, depending on what was available. Milk, eggs, and dried fruit were hard to get hold of and as such were optional in most cake recipes. Also, as women turned to baking bread at home, they often struggled to source yeast because it was in such high demand. As a result, they came up with a recipe for Crazy Dough or Wonder Dough, used in a variety of sweet and savory bread recipes over and over again. A small ball of wonder dough from the first batch was kept in a plastic bag in the refrigerator for up to seven days. This starter dough served as a rising agent instead of yeast in the next round of baking.

The names of the new foodstuffs signaled that these were not ordinary recipes. Their names were chosen to distinguish such recipes from one's normal diet as a collective reminder that the use of these recipes, just like the overall societal situation, was only temporary. There was an underlying irony in the way these people described the foods they made with fewer ingredients as being "from nothing." This self-deprecating attitude toward changes in food consumption brought on by austerity functioned as a buffer for coping with extreme and rapid changes in society and (home) economy.

Irony has found its place in many societies as a means of making sense of contradictions or extreme situations. However, many varieties of irony can encode different attitudes toward social experience, or, as Alan Wilde puts it, different "horizons of assent."[15] While Michael Herzfeld argues that use of irony among Greeks "may contribute more to the perpetuation than to the eradication of a sense of grievance and victimage," in James Clifford's view, irony is "an ideology of order, or perhaps of acceptable disorder."[16] Clifford's understanding of the use of irony as a search for stability is instrumental in analyzing the irony in discourse about food in Serbia during the 1990s. It is not surprising, then, to learn that almost none of the recipes from the 1990s are still used today; in most cases, it took my research participants a long time to locate these recipes in their cookbooks, showing that the recipes had long since been abandoned. The war recipes and cookbooks from twenty years ago have been replaced with regular recipes requiring abundantly available and diverse ingredients. Even though many of my informants complained of the continued economic crisis in Serbia, and some of them confessed that they were forced to bake bread at home because it was cheaper, no one used the war recipes any longer. If they did sometimes bake a cake with similar ingredients to the eponymous Embargo Cake, they gave it a different name (Easy Fruit Cake or Cake with Apples), thereby affirming that, despite ongoing economic difficulties, life had returned to normal compared to the situation twenty years earlier.

Grow Your Own

In addition to home baking, women also resorted to using whatever vegetables and fruits they could buy in food markets.[17] At that time, fruit and vegetables were commonly sold in *pijace*—food markets where farmers from nearby villages sold their produce. During hyperinflation, producers tied the prices of their food to the deutsche mark (German mark) and adjusted the prices throughout the day. The problem with this strategy was that people's salaries were not in line with hyperinflation. As a result, by the time shoppers got to the market, all they could buy with their pay was a couple of eggs or a kilo of potatoes. Even though fruit and vegetables were available at green markets, most people could not afford them unless they had foreign currency savings to spend on food.

For this reason, people frequently used any piece of land they had to grow their own vegetables. Jovanka, the university professor from Belgrade quoted in the previous section, had a sister who lived in a house in Belgrade. During the hyperinflation period, Jovanka's sister dug out the flowers from a small front garden outside her home and planted vegetables there instead.

The majority of people in Belgrade lived in apartment buildings, not houses, so this option was not always available to them. However, because many city dwellers were among the first generation of their families to leave the countryside, they still maintained strong ties to their villages, returning every weekend to take part in farming alongside their relatives.[18] Others had *placevi* (plots) near Belgrade where they grew fruit and vegetables. The main obstacle in both cases was access to villages and plots, as gasoline was only available on the black market at a highly inflated price of five deutsche marks per liter (roughly USD 2.70 per liter). Those who could not afford the gasoline to commute to their village or *plac* every weekend relied on skeleton bus services, overcrowded with passengers.

Stana recalled an anecdote from one of these trips to the *plac* that she owned and tended alongside her late husband:

> It was summer 1993, and my husband and I wanted to go to our plot to harvest garden peas. However, there was no bus service to the village where we had the plot because of [lack of] gasoline, and we had to take an alternative route that involved an hour's walk from the bus stop to the village. It was a hot, sticky day, and I was wearing a summer dress and sandals. The bus that we were on was so overcrowded that by the time I got out of the bus, the elastic band on my knickers snapped and they fell off as I got off the bus! And then we had another hour on foot to get to the village. By the time we got there, my sandals were entirely torn and destroyed.[19]

Stana lived with her husband, son, daughter, and granddaughter in a one-bedroom apartment in New Belgrade. She worked as a seamstress for the army, and her salary was so low that she could not even afford to buy a bag of potatoes with it during hyperinflation. Growing her own vegetables at any cost—including episodes like this, torn sandals, lost underwear, and all—was the only available solution she saw to feed her family. Because she grew up in a village in the mountains, Stana possessed extensive knowledge about foraging, growing, and preparing food. She had seven brothers, and as the only daughter she was expected to cook, clean, and tend livestock from a very early age. Stana learned to bake bread and pies before the age of six, and her mother taught her about the wild foods they collected from the forest. She was familiar with wild mushrooms and knew which ones were safe to eat; she also harvested nettles and used them to make soups. Rosehips, blackberries, hawthorn berries, and cherry plums were just some of the wild foods that Stana picked from a forest near her plot and used to make jams and concentrated fruit juices.

Stana was one of several informants who took pride in possessing knowledge about wild foods, as well as in the ability to use this knowledge to feed their families in ways they considered healthier than merely cooking with flour three times a day. Like Stana, Borka also had extensive knowledge about wild foods and foraging.[20] Borka was a bank manager in the 1990s, and from Monday to Friday, she was dedicated to her professional career. During weekends, however, Borka went back to her village to help her family. Borka's mother and sister lived in a village in southwestern Serbia. Her family was well off and owned about ten hectares of land in and around the village. Before the communists seized power, Borka explained, her family had much more land, and theirs was one of the wealthiest villages in Serbia. The communists, however, only allowed them to keep ten hectares and nationalized their remaining property. Even though Borka did not live in the village, she continued to help her relatives and participate in seasonal agricultural work. Borka went to Bulgaria and Romania to buy seeds and salt for her family and the neighbors in the village, since these items were difficult to obtain during the hyperinflation period. Because her family had no agricultural machinery and just owned the land, they had a *napola* agreement with their village neighbors. In practice, this meant that their neighbors did all the machinery-related work and in return received half of all the crops from Borka's family's land. Borka and her family reciprocated by taking part in their neighbors' seasonal work.

In addition to growing her own wheat, corn, vegetables, and fruit, Borka foraged the woods for wild herbs and foods. Nettles, in Borka's view, had superior health and dietary properties compared to spinach, and she preferred them to cultivated leafy greens. Borka used the opportunity to emphasize the poor quality of food her migrant daughter Lea and her family in Toronto consumed—"Spinach in Canada has no taste or smell, as if it isn't spinach!"

Once again, the transmission of knowledge of farming and foraging gained from preindustrial life helped women grow their own food and source wild foods safe for consumption. Because of the rapid industrialization that took place in the former Yugoslavia after World War II, many facets of preindustrial life were well preserved, and practices from the preindustrial period coexisted with industrialized Yugoslav society in the period 1945–91. One's know-how in farming and foraging, extended family connections with those who still farmed, a return to lard (over industrial oils), relearning how to bake—all pointed to a preindustrial lifestyle.

People survived the UN sanctions and hyperinflation as this not-too-distant knowledge and skill set was reinvigorated and reintroduced. This knowledge was transmitted intergenerationally through those who experienced war, poverty, and scarcity, as well as intragenerationally through the experience of industrial and preindustrial worlds existing side by side in postwar Serbia. Despite Josip Broz Tito's efforts to reform the preindustrial way of life in Yugoslavia after 1945, it persisted alongside industrialized consumer society, often creating paradoxes of modern life in the former Yugoslavia.[21] This explains the irony and self-deprecating attitude of citizens during the UN embargo: people made fun of their surreal everyday lives because they possessed survival skills and knowledge that helped them circumvent the crisis. Instead of becoming helpless victims of halted consumerism, they turned to re-creating ways of producing and sourcing food for their needs. Irony and self-mockery served as a reminder that this was yet another paradox associated with inhabiting a simultaneously modern and premodern society. Irony also separated this "carnivalesque" period from "normal" or "regular" life.[22]

However, not everyone in Belgrade had relatives in the countryside or plots where they could grow their own food—or even the knowledge of how to grow things. These people relied heavily on their social networks, a considerable source of the capital that enabled survival during the worst period of hyperinflation in the early 1990s. In the next section, we analyze these social networks and the way people used them for survival.

Social Networks

Natalija worked as a clinical doctor in the 1990s.[23] She lived in a one-bedroom apartment in New Belgrade with her husband, Voja, also a doctor, and their two children: one in secondary school at the time, and the other a university student in the mid-1990s. Natalija recalled the shock she experienced when the embargo turned the familiar into the unrecognizable overnight: "Before the sanctions, there was everything. I remember walking past the shop window in Knez Mihajlova [a pedestrian street in the heart of Belgrade's city center] and looking at Mozartkugel chocolates; they were expensive, and I could not afford them, but it was a feast [for the eyes] to see them. This abundance of food followed by such scarcity was shocking. It was so confusing to see empty shelves everywhere. For my whole monthly salary, that of a specialist clinical doctor, all I could buy was three eggs."

Unlike many other city dwellers, Natalija and her husband did not have relatives in the countryside to help them with food. Also, unlike the majority of socialist companies that had trade unions to supply their workers with food during the crisis, the doctors' union was not as efficient, so there was no help with food from that source either. But there was solidarity among people, conceded Natalija. One friend who worked for the government brought them rice once. Also, Natalija recalled, she had a cousin, a refugee from Croatia, who settled in a village close to the Danube north of Belgrade. This cousin once brought them a basket filled with beans and homemade jams that he and his wife had made. "I will never forget the sight of my cousin carrying this old washing basket filled with foods we could only dream of then," reflected Natalija.

As this recollection demonstrates, the economic changes were rapid, and "subsistence networks" consisting of family, friends, neighbors, and work colleagues became vital in securing food.[24] The better connected one was, the more likely one could obtain food or information about its availability. In 1990s Serbia, social networks provided people with food and furthermore offered a broad range of services as a replacement for failed institutional support. This is not to say that social networks did not exist before the 1990s. On the contrary, people relied on their social networks through previous crises during the time of Yugoslavia. Research from the 1980s demonstrates the importance of social networks among women in socialist Yugoslavia.[25] Women relied on these contacts for support in securing a place in a desirable kindergarten for their child, for obtaining goods that were in short supply, for securing financial credit or loans, or for accessing medical services.[26] However, the severity of the 1990s crisis—in which economic collapse was compounded with the crumbling of socialist institutions and the war in the region—contributed to the unprecedented strengthening of, and dependency on, social networks.

This exchange of services and food between friends and relatives in post-1990s Belgrade also bears many similarities to such exchanges in Moscow during the same period, Romania during the last decade of communism, and Argentina during several crisis periods in the 1990s and early 2000s.[27] Describing the phenomenon of exchange in Russia, Melissa Caldwell argues that it could not be classified as a traditional exchange, in which a relationship between the parties involved exists only during the exchange, nor does it conform to the classic Maussian gift exchange pattern, wherein a receiver is expected to reciprocate within a particular time frame.[28] Exchanges in this traditional context exist prior to sociality, and people actually use exchanges to sustain relationships.[29] Instances of exchange in postcommunist Serbia, Russia, and Argentina presuppose the existence of a relationship prior to any exchange. Caldwell argues that in postcommunist Russia, "acts of exchange verify and concretize existing social relations and the trust that exists between partners."[30] Likewise, in the case of Argentina, Patricia Aguirre notes that "reciprocity reinforces and/or maintains existing social links between friends, neighbors, and/or family members."[31]

As we have seen, exchanges in post-1990 Serbia took place within a social network that consisted of family, friends, colleagues, and neighbors. Moreover, as much as kinship relationships were revived and mobilized in the postcommunist period as a substitute for the collapse of institutions and institutional support, other elements of social networks—such as relationships with friends, colleagues, and neighbors—became a complementary source of capital. Personal networks filled the vacuum created by the collapse of socialism and the slow and reluctant emergence of new post-socialist state institutions. The wider and stronger one's social network was, the more capital one possessed. It may not have been possible or necessary to bank on that capital immediately, but by keeping a relationship active, one was able to hold on to a bond whose value would not change with time. Carolyn Stevens aptly terms these personal connections as "deposits in [the] favor bank."[32]

The example of Jovanka, the university professor, is a good illustration of this point. Jovanka noted that people helped one another during hyperinflation in a way that has not occurred since: "There was a lot of solidarity at work. We exchanged our salaries from dinars to [German] marks, going to street currency dealers together to get a better rate, and if there wasn't enough small change to divide the salaries, we didn't mind paying more to someone because next time someone else would be in that situation. Today, many of those colleagues can't see eye to eye with one another, but a memory of that solidarity is still there."

This ad hoc social security system, however, was not predicated on direct reciprocity: Natalija had no obligation to return gifts to her friends or relatives, nor was Jovanka obligated, within any particular time frame, to return even a single German mark to the colleague with whom she had split her converted salary. This (relative) freedom of debt was what Natalija and many other research participants termed *solidarnost* (solidarity). Although people helped others in their social network without expecting a direct return of the favor, this did not cancel their debt. Debts remained a necessary component of the social network, and as such they could be considered a social network tax. *Solidarnost* was the only way to release oneself from this type of debt morally. In other words, solidarism was maintained by keeping up with regular payments of social network tax.

Natalija, Jovanka, and many other research participants emphasized the difference between the 2000s and the period of economic hardship in the 1990s, noting that solidarity among people no longer existed when I was interviewing them. One can dismiss this view as a nostalgic, rose-tinted view of the past. But it can also be argued that instances of solidarity experienced in the 1990s were typical of the extraordinary socioeconomic situation in Serbia. As the economic crisis eased, pressure on social networks as "subsistence networks" gradually lessened; in turn, the favors, and the debts incurred by those favors, became smaller.[33] This effectively led to a decrease in solidarity because the social network tax was much lower. What changed was not people's morality or humanity but the size and effectiveness of social networks that operated with reduced capacity.

Food Scarcity and Hunger

During my encounters with people who shared their experiences about securing and preparing food during the 1990s, one of the first things my informants pointed out was that despite the situation in the country, "people were not hungry" ("*narod nije bio gladan*"). People acknowledged that diets lacked variety and that everything was made primarily of flour, but they also felt the need to emphasize that they had not been starving. Hunger was something they associated with their childhood years during World War II, whereas in the 1990s, according to my research participants, hunger mainly affected people in war-torn Bosnia-Herzegovina and those on the margins of society. Several people remarked that memories of hunger from World War II probably drove their obsession with stocking up on staples, bordering on hoarding practices, during the 1990s; they wanted to protect their children from experiencing hunger as they had.

When I remarked that in the 1990s, one started to notice people rummaging through trash bins in Belgrade, my informants conceded that this was unprecedented and that indeed there must have been people forced to look for food in the garbage, but they did not personally know anyone who did this. Some suggested that it was mainly the Roma population or elderly pensioners in Belgrade who searched trash bins for food. However, some of the Roma research participants I worked with noted that they were not hungry either during the 1990s because they worked for the Mafia selling smuggled cigarettes and had no problem feeding their families. I do not mean to imply that all the Roma people were engaged in illicit activities during the 1990s or that illicit groups were exclusively employing the Roma. Black marketers were indiscriminate in recruiting workers from all segments of society.

The black market flourished in the 1990s in response to the official trade ban imposed by UN sanctions. Ironically, for some people in Belgrade, including for some members of the traditionally marginalized Roma population, smuggling and black market trading provided a higher income than in the prewar years. The Mafia bosses who employed the Roma population to hawk smuggled goods on the streets were good employers, according to my informant Boban, who worked for them during the 1990s.[34] Unlike traditional work settings, where one needed a *debela veza* (powerful connection) to get a job and where the Roma were often discriminated against, those in the Mafia had different requirements. One could choose what he wanted to sell—toilet paper, cigarettes, gasoline—and if one worked hard, he was paid regularly and well protected. If a hawker tried to pull any tricks, Boban explained, he would get a bullet in the head.

Boban, a Serbian Roma, lived with his wife and four children on the outskirts of Belgrade. He remembered the 1990s as a period of prosperity because the Mafia paid him regularly and in foreign currency. This regular salary enabled him to start building a house for his family in 1997. "When no one had anything," explained Boban, "we did well because the cigarette-smuggling business was thriving."

The Roma who lived in villages outside Belgrade, however, were in a much more difficult situation. In the late 1990s, Boban bumped into his wife's cousin from the countryside begging on the streets of Belgrade. The cousin was embarrassed but explained that there was no work and no food in his village. Boban then put him in touch with his Mafia bosses and convinced him to sell toilet paper for them, along with other Roma from the same village.

This trope of elusive hunger in 1990s Serbia is not dissimilar to Caldwell's descriptions of Moscow in the same period. While many Muscovites claimed there was no hunger in Russia, the regular sight of people begging for food on the streets of Moscow hinted at a different reality.[35]

According to Caldwell, "food poverty is a social, not an economic, condition; and it is those individuals without social connections who are at greatest risk of lacking *access* to food and thereby go hungry."[36] In the case of Belgrade in the 1990s, even traditionally marginalized groups in Serbian society, like the Roma, were sheltered from hunger if they belonged to a social network. Those who were outside networks of support, however, fared the worst. A striking and tragic case in point were the deaths of seventy patients in a psychiatric hospital, Gornja Toponica, near Niš in the south of Serbia. The patients died over the course of ten days due to lack of medicine, heating, and food.[37]

Simply put, those who were outside the systems of social networks and support and those dependent on institutional care, such as the severely ill, were hit hardest by food poverty and material deprivation. Those who were part of a social group were taken care of, even if individually they had insufficient material means of support. Membership in a social network, however, required considerable effort and active participation in sharing information, care, and resources, as well as abiding by specific moral norms. As with the Muscovites' sense of morality, their counterparts in Belgrade knew what was appropriate—or not. When Boban brought his wife's cousin into the smuggling business, he relied on the cousin's help, along with the help of other relatives and neighbors from the cousin's village, in hawking cigarettes when necessary (even though their designated goods were rolls of toilet paper). The cousin knew this was his lifeline and agreed to help out because Boban had helped him previously by giving him an opportunity to trade on the black market.

Memories of Hunger

Despite many people's insistence that they were not hungry during the 1990s, the trope of hunger was nevertheless present in people's everyday lives. Stana recalled that the first sign of food scarcity in the early 1990s pushed her into a "fight-or-flight mode" because it brought back memories of starvation from childhood. Stana was born in 1940 in a mountain village in the south of Serbia, and her childhood hardship had a profound influence on her adult life:

> We were starving. Our house was burned down during the war [World War II]; we were refugees. I was the only girl in the family, and my mother taught me to make bread and pies at the age of five. I also helped my mother with lambing

from this early age. That is where the fear of hunger stemmed from, as well as the need to always have a stocked-up pantry as a shield against hunger. That's why [in the 1990s], wherever I saw a notice in a shop that the following day they would have this or that in stock, I always queued up. When I finally got to the front of the queue, goods were usually gone. I caught pneumonia three times from waiting in lines for bread and milk [in the 1990s]. I sacrificed myself to provide my children with what I didn't have [growing up].

Stana had a son in his early twenties and a daughter in her late teens in the early 1990s. Her daughter, Ivana, had a baby while in high school but continued living with Stana after the birth. Ivana had a very different mind-set regarding the food lines than her mother. She was twenty in 1993 when hyperinflation peaked—a young mother with a two-year-old baby—and decided against going to university, as she saw no point in pursuing higher education when it could not guarantee better opportunities in life: "When I saw doctors and other educated people smuggling goods from Bulgaria alongside us, I realized there was no point spending time studying when I'd end up selling tuna cans on the street just like them. My friends and I were not buying into the victim story and this whole '*logorsko ponašanje*' [camp behavior] of constantly waiting in lines.[38] We lived in the moment. We went to Bulgaria to buy beer, not cheese. We had no plans for the future because we didn't see any future."[39]

Ivana's brother, Marko, was twenty-three in 1993 and worked night shifts in a fast-food joint selling burgers. According to Marko, he was earning more than a surgeon at the time. The restaurant's revenue came not only from selling burgers but also from dealing in foreign currency: customers would often pay in German marks and receive change in dinars. At that time, few (fast- or otherwise) food outlets were open during the night in Belgrade. The particular location of Marko's eatery guaranteed regular, hungry customers: "At the start of my night shift, the first customers were the soldiers because we were close to the army barracks, followed by the policemen, and the last ones at dawn were the criminals."[40] Like his sister, Ivana, Marko also noted that women—"housewives," as he described them—felt the scarcity more than anyone else. His younger generation did not participate in "the system of flour, sugar, and oil procurement." "People were spreading despair in those lines; that's why they waited in queues," explained Marko. "The Serbs' biggest fear is the fear of hunger."

The difference in people's reactions to food scarcity in the 1990s depended on their age and experience of hunger. The younger generations, born in the 1960s and 1970s, were more relaxed than their parents' generation because they had no memories of hunger and deprivation. Moreover, the young had the luxury of not worrying about where their bread would come from because they knew their mothers, grandmothers, and aunts were there to look after them.

As we have seen with Stana, mothers in Serbia considered it their duty to provide for their children and grandchildren long into their adulthood. It was common to find several generations living in small, one-bedroom apartments. To look after and provide for one's children and their families was what Serbian mothers did. None of my informants questioned this; they considered it their duty, which everyone, including themselves, took for granted. Feeding work, according to Marjorie DeVault, is "one of the primary ways that women 'do' gender." By feeding the family, "a woman conducts herself as recognizably womanly."[41] Despite notable differences between the American women in DeVault's study and the Serbian women in this book, there is a strong parallel between the social construction of women as providers and pillars of the family. Like their American counterparts, Serbian mothers were socialized into their roles as women and mothers through the work they performed for their children and families. Despite the emancipation achieved through education and employment during socialism, women operated within the normative structure of Serbian patriarchal society. Rapid urbanization in the postwar period did not dismantle the public-private gender dichotomy.[42] Social research from socialist Yugoslavia shows that despite equal opportunities for education and employment, women were marginalized in the public sphere with very low participation in well-paid managerial positions and the governing sector, despite their initial breakthrough during World War II.[43] While women were more likely to migrate from rural to urban areas in the postwar period and take advantage of the opportunities for education and employment, once employed they rarely progressed in their careers.[44] Women made up for this lack of opportunity and recognition in the public sphere through their domestic work—as homemakers and mothers. Even if not entirely satisfied with their family arrangements, women compensated with having children, giving them someone to care for and watch grow up.[45] And just as in DeVault's study, this work went mostly unacknowledged; it was taken for granted that this was what women were supposed to do as women. Migration complicated this relationship dynamic, particularly for those who left in the 1990s at the time of severe economic crisis, scarcity, and hyperinflation. Mothers did not know how to react to gifts from their migrant children. On the one hand, they were moved to see their children come home loaded with gifts "like Father Christmas," as one of my informants described her son, who came to visit her from America in 1993 carrying laundry detergent, soaps, shampoos, canned food, rice, and pasta. Yet, on the other hand, these mothers felt like they had failed their children because they could not provide for them. This sense of failure in one's role of mother (and grandmother) underlined all forms of exchange between mothers and their migrant children. Mothers had a strong desire to reverse this by making vicarious sacrifices and depriving themselves of everything they could for the sake of providing for their children and grandchildren. They might have lived for a week on cabbage, followed by a week on bean soup, for months on end, but when their migrant children came to visit, they prepared feasts for them from ingredients they had squirreled away over the previous months of deprivation. Likewise, they would often try to find a way to send a birthday gift to grandchildren abroad, usually chocolates and money, both of which were hard to get in Serbia at that time.

Hunger, their efforts show, was a trope that had no place in a mother's world. Mothers considered it their mission to shield their families from starvation. If this meant that they had to go hungry to achieve their self-imposed task of feeding others, it was a price they were willing to pay. Hunger afflicted those who had no one to shelter them. Mothers might have been hungry but would not admit it—this went against societal expectations of what it meant to be a mother and a woman. Their hunger was satiated vicariously by ensuring that those who depended on them were fed and provided for. This was their victory in the locust years.

Notes

1. The phrase "locust years" is found in the Bible in the passage Joel 2:25–32. This is also a title of a chapter in Winston Churchill's multivolume book about the Second World War and its build up. Finally, a Serbian writer Borislav Pekić published a book with the same title. The phrase has with time slipped away from a narrow literary meaning and used to describe economic hardship.

2. Pekić, *Godine koje su pojeli skakavci* [The years the locusts have devoured]; Čerčil [Churchill], *Drugi svetski rat* [The Second World War].

3. Simić, *Peasant Urbanites.*

4. Pavličić, *Kruh i mast* [Bread and lard], 7. All translations in this text are by the author unless otherwise noted.

5. Ibid.

6. Lola, interview by author, Belgrade, February 11, 2014.

7. See, for example, articles about the rise in popularity of home baking in the last ten years in the United Kingdom: Mesure, "Feeling Kneady"; Roux, "Great British Food Revival"; and Jones, "The Great British Bake Graph!"

8. Seremetakis, "The Memory of the Senses," 9.

9. Following years of advice against animal fat consumption in favor of olive and coconut oil, a different approach to lard has started to emerge in recent years: Hinde, "Vegetable Oil Linked to Cancer"; Moss, "Lard May Be Healthier"; Thring, "Consider Lard"; Mosley, "Why It's Healthier to Cook with Lard."

10. Jelena Radulović published *Ratni Kuvar* [War cookbook] in 1942. See also Jugoslovenska Narodna Armija (JNA), *Uputstvo o pripremanju jela u JNA u ratu* [A manual for food preparation].

11. Jovanka, interview by author, Belgrade, February 15, 2014.

12. Barth, "An Anthropology of Knowledge," 1.

13. The people who took part in this research were mainly in their forties and fifties during the early to mid-1990s. The majority were employed and coped much better than the elderly or the sick, for example, whose survival was seriously endangered by the combination of hyperinflation and the UN embargo.

14. UNPROFOR is the acronym for the United Nations Protection Force, the first UN peacekeeping force in Croatia and Bosnia-Herzegovina during the war in the former Yugoslavia.

15. Wilde, *Horizons of Assent*.

16. Herzfeld, "Irony and Power," 77; Clifford, "The Last Discussant," 256.

17. Although the title of this section may be reminiscent of the "grow your own, can your own" slogan and the British "Dig for Victory" campaign during World War II, efforts to grow one's food in 1990s Serbia had nothing to do with any state-sponsored propaganda. These were solely individual efforts to bring food to the table.

18. In 1989, Belgrade had more than 1.6 million inhabitants, but only one-third of its population had been born there (Kaser, Familie und Verwandtschaft, 427, cited in Kaser, *Patriarchy After Patriarchy*, 121). This suggests that family relationships between those living in the city and those in the countryside were quite strong, particularly during the sanctions in the early 1990s, when townspeople relied much more on help with food from their relatives in the country (Matić, "Urban Economies," 144).

19. Stana, interview by author, Belgrade, February 6, 2014.

20. Borka, interview by author, Belgrade, February 9, 2014.

21. Tito was a leader of Socialist Yugoslavia, serving in various governing roles from 1943 to 1980. For more recent descriptions of the rural-urban paradox in Serbia, see Matić, "Urban Economies." Andrei Simić's 1973 ethnography, *The Peasant Urbanites*, is a classic in this field.

22. Carnival, according to Bakhtin, is all encompassing: everyone is a participant, there are no observers, and "there is no life outside it." Life during carnival is subject only to its own laws, no other rules or laws apply during that period. Bakhtin, *Rabelais and His World*, 7.

23. Natalija, interview by author, Belgrade, February 10, 2014.

24. "Subsistence networks" is a term by Perianu, "Précarité Alimentaire, Austérité" [Food insecurity and austerity], cited in Guidonet Riera, *The Spanish Civil War*.

25. Milić, "Žene u bivšoj Jugoslaviji" [Women in former Yugoslavia].

26. Milić, "Socijalna mreža porodičnih odnosa" [Social Strata and Social Networks of Family Relation], 111–57, cited in Milić, "Žene u bivšoj Jugoslaviji," 195.

27. For Russia, see Humphrey, "Creating a Culture of Disillusionment," Humphrey and Mandel, *Market and Moralities*, and Caldwell, *Not by Bread Alone*; for Romania, see Perianu, "Précarité Alimentaire, Austérité"; and for Argentina, see Aguirre, *Estrategias de Consume* [Consumption strategies].

28. Sahlins, *Stone Age Economics*, cited in Caldwell, *Not by Bread Alone*, 98.

29. Bourdieu, *Outline of a Theory of Practice*; Mauss, *The Gift*, cited in Caldwell, *Not by Bread Alone*, 99.

30. Caldwell, *Not by Bread Alone*, 99.

31. Aguirre, *Estrategias de Consume*, 125, cited in Guidonet Riera, *The Spanish Civil War*, 102. Translation by Guidonet Riera.

32. Stevens, *On the Margins of Japanese Society*, 231, cited in Caldwell, *Not by Bread Alone*, 98.

33. "Subsistence networks" term by Perianu, "Précarité Alimentaire, Austérité," cited in Guidonet Riera, *The Spanish Civil War*, 101. Translation by Guidonet Riera.

34. Boban, interview by author, Belgrade, February 14, 2014.

35. Caldwell, *Not by Bread Alone*, 157–58.

36. Ibid., 167 (emphasis in original).

37. Todorović, "Dnevno umire desetak bolesnika" [Ten patients die daily], 1.

38. The phrase "logorsko ponašanje" referred to people behaving like they were in a concentration camp—fenced off from the rest of the world, unable to leave, and awaiting death.

39. Ivana, interview by author, Belgrade, February 8, 2014.

40. Marko, interview by author, Belgrade, February 8, 2014.

41. DeVault, *Feeding the Family*, 118.

42. Denich, "Urbanization and Women's Role"; Milić, "Žene u bivšoj Jugoslaviji" [Women in former Yugoslavia].

43. Božinović, "Žene u modernizacijskim procesima" [Women in modernization processes], cited in Milić, "Žene u bivšoj Jugoslaviji" [Women in former Yugoslavia], 190. Milić notes that during World War II about one million women took part in military and civilian activities of the People's Liberation Movement (*Narodno-oslobodilački pokret*). This high involvement of women, however, halted in the postwar period, with patriarchal norms taking precedence over women's breakthrough into the public sphere.

44. Bogdanović, "Materijalni standard društvenih slojeva" [Standard of living of social strata], 519.

45. Burić, Pešić, Milić, Milosavljević, Vujović, Nemanjić, *Porodica i društveni sistem* [Family and a social system]; Blagojević, "Mladi i roditeljstvo" [Youth and parenthood].

2

A BITE OF YUGOSLAVIA

Food, Memory, and Migration

FOOD WAS VITAL IN MOTHERS' ATTEMPTS TO KEEP in touch with their migrant children and their families. It was a medium for expressing their emotions for loved ones far away. Familiar food from Yugoslavia provided comfort and continuity for some of the post-1990 migrants as well, helping them navigate a difficult period of settling in their new destination countries while their home country—along with their familiar world—was falling apart. For other post-Yugoslav migrants, their relationship with food from home was more complicated, contributing to tension with their families in Serbia. Despite these differences between migrants' and mothers' feelings toward food from home, food was instrumental for migrants and their families left behind not only because it helped restore a sense of wholeness ruptured by migration and the collapse of Yugoslavia but also because it was an expression of the relationship between them and their subjectivity.[1]

While most studies about food and migration focus on the significance of food for migrants, we know comparatively little about the food sent by families left behind.[2] This chapter explores why sending food from home was significant to mothers left behind and what these practices meant to them.

Taste of Home

Mothers left behind, as I discovered in my research, are affected by a sense of rupture and loss, just like migrants. The wars and their ripple effects spanned the entirety of the last decade of the twentieth century in Serbia. Young women and men who left the country in the early 1990s could not return to visit for several years. Escaping military conscription, staying illegally in a new country, not being able to afford overseas plane tickets, or sometimes not wanting to confront the place and the people they had left behind were some of the reasons mothers had not seen their adult sons and daughters for some time. On the other side, mothers often could not afford to travel or secure visas to visit the countries where their children lived. Food sent to children abroad was thus one of the few ways for mothers to stay connected with their children.

When I met Radoslava in 2005, she was living in a one-bedroom apartment in the center of Belgrade.[3] She was a retired textile designer and had a son and a daughter from two marriages. Her son, Miloš, emigrated to Canada in 1993, fleeing conscription for the war front in Croatia. Shortly before he left, Miloš had graduated with a degree in architecture and had started to work for a big construction company in Belgrade that sponsored his studies. However, he was repeatedly receiving calls to report to the army, and his mother stepped in to help Miloš leave the country and escape the war. She had asked a relative in France to send him an invitation letter, which was necessary for a visa application. Miloš secured a tourist visa for France, crossing the Serbian border with Hungary at the last moment before a new law, in support of mandatory military conscription, banned men between eighteen and sixty-five from leaving the country. He found a job immediately as an architect in Paris. But without a work permit, and not wanting to work illegally, he returned to Belgrade.

Miloš spent several months in Belgrade hiding from the military police and sleeping at friends' homes while sorting out the papers for immigration to Canada. Six months later, he received a Canadian visa but still had to find $10,000 to put toward a deposit into his bank account as proof to Canadian immigration authorities that he would have the means to support himself upon arrival. He sold all his possessions—his vinyl records, stereo, and car—and his mother gave him the remaining amount. Following his settlement in Canada, his long-term girlfriend joined him six months later. They got married and soon had two children. According to Radoslava, it was not easy for her son in the beginning, but his ambition and hard work quickly started to yield results. She helped him as well: following the death of Miloš's father, Radoslava sold his late father's apartment and sent the money to her son to use toward a deposit for a house he wanted to buy for his family.

Radoslava was somewhat younger, healthier, and financially better off than most of the other mothers I met, enabling her to physically and financially travel. Although she could afford to visit her son, Radoslava struggled to get a travel visa to Canada. The immigration authorities at the Canadian consulate in Belgrade were reluctant to grant her permission to see her son, as their records showed that Miloš had also invited his girlfriend on a tourist visa, and she had then stayed on in Canada and married him. Despite these problems, Radoslava eventually received a visitor visa and went to see her son and his family in Toronto in 1995, two years after he had emigrated. However, she did not have a good relationship with her daughter-in-law. Radoslava had advised her daughter-in-law against marrying Miloš, as they had been arguing a lot even before their marriage. It was no surprise, then, that Radoslava was not too welcome in her son's home.

Radoslava's *prija* (daughter-in-law's mother) went on a tourist visa to look after the grandchildren, while Radoslava could only stay for shorter periods because of the tension between her and her daughter-in-law. Radoslava was concerned that her grandsons were becoming fat because of the fast food provided by their mother and their other grandmother. To make the children happy, Radoslava remarked with a tinge of resentment, their other grandmother cooked the unhealthy junk food that children in Canada liked to eat—meatballs, fries, and pancakes. When she went to stay with them, Radoslava cooked healthier foods for her grandchildren, but she spent much less time with her son's family compared to the other grandmother, who was seemingly more concerned with her grandchildren enjoying their food than feeding them healthy meals. Radoslava concluded regrettably that the years had taken their toll, quoting a Serbian saying: "Far from the eyes, far from the heart."[4] In the past, she explained, they kept in touch more regularly, adding bitterly, "Not only does my son call less often, but they also don't want food from here; my grandsons prefer Canadian junk food to my cooking." The rejection of a mother's food, as this example shows, marks a more severe fracture in the relationship with her son and grandchildren than fewer phone calls.

Food communicates at a much deeper level because of its sensory qualities, which trigger personal memories. This relationship between food and memory has been immortalized in Marcel Proust's epic novel *In Search of Lost Time*.[5] A bite of a quaint *madeleine* could conjure a scene from one's childhood so vividly: the smell of tea in which the soft biscuit was dipped, the sounds from a nearby church and square, the streets, the people—all this came to life in a single sensory experience. Even without having read

Proust's lengthy novel, mothers were fully aware that as long as their grand-children and children were eating their food, they would be remembered. The last thing mothers wanted to hear was that their food was not welcome anymore, particularly when the reason given was that the food had become too heavy for their stomachs. Mothers were very hurt by this repudiation, feeling it implied that they did not know what was good for their children and grandchildren.

Nothing else held the same significance as sending food or cooking when visiting. When Radoslava's son asked his mother to send him his old books and catalogs from architecture exhibitions in Belgrade, she did what he asked, but she did not hide her resentment: "There was no point keeping them, as he was clearly not coming back." The books and printed materials that her son had asked her to send played no role in keeping in touch or being close. For Radoslava, only the consumption of food that she brought them or cooked while visiting could create a close relationship and bond with her son and grandchildren. The rejection of her food was a clear sign for Radoslava that their relationship was not as close as it had been in the past. While not all mothers of migrant children in Serbia had the same experience as Radoslava, as exemplified by her *prija* who cooked fast food for her grandchildren, it was nevertheless quite common for mothers to note that with their migrant children's loss of interest in their food, their relationship became more distant.

Migrant children's changing food tastes and loss of interest in some Serbian food products was particularly hurtful to parents. When children asked mothers to stop sending certain foods because they found them too heavy or greasy, mothers interpreted it as a repudiation not only of their gift but of themselves as well.[6] Families, as DeVault has argued, are constructed through daily activities that bring them together.[7] The person who cooks for the family—usually a woman—constructs "her own place within the family, as one who provides for the needs of others."[8] The experiences of Belgrade mothers support the constructivist view of the family: when there are no family members to provide for, there is no family and, ultimately, no mother either. One becomes a mother by doing activities that a mother is expected to do for her children. When children reject her role, the moth-er's identity is called into question. As examples in this book show, not all mothers passively surrender their identity. There are different degrees of involvement and strategies to preserve this identity, even when children do not want to be mothered anymore.

Gorica and Valentina provide another example of changes in food consumption as indicative of changes in a mother-child relationship.[9] Valentina graduated with a degree in electrical engineering in Belgrade in the early 1990s. Top grades and a scholarship from a large construction company could not help Valentina find a job in Serbia, however. Her boyfriend at the time had contact with a professor in Lisbon, and the two of them decided to go to Portugal and try their luck there. Valentina did not plan to stay there longer than a month, but as the situation in Serbia deteriorated and her chances of employment diminished, Valentina started looking for a job in Portugal. She soon found a job at a telecommunications company. Valentina was an only child, and her mother, Gorica, took it hard when she realized her daughter was not coming back. Despite a span of more than ten years, Gorica could vividly recall the events that marked her daughter's departure:

> She left on December 15, 1992, with only one small suitcase. No one knew she would stay there for good. I couldn't visit her the next year. A year and four months passed until I saw my daughter again. I went to Portugal to see my Valentina on March 31, 1994, and stayed with her for a month. That was the first time since I gave birth to my daughter that I hadn't seen her for so long. You should have seen our encounter at the airport: I was waiting for my luggage to appear on the belt, and then I saw her on the other side of the glass window. I forgot about the bags and rushed to hug her; I was so excited to see my girl again that I hit the window glass and broke my spectacles. The policemen were staring in awe, not understanding what had happened.

After that, Gorica saw her daughter every year. Gorica spent even more time with them after Valentina had a child. However, the relationship between mother and daughter gradually transformed. In the early 2000s, Valentina married a Belgian man and moved from Portugal to Belgium. Gorica noted how her daughter's food preferences had changed since she emigrated, not hiding her disappointment with Valentina's change in taste: "In the first years, I was always carrying *kajmak* for her; nowadays, however, she doesn't want *kajmak* anymore; when she was here last time, she didn't even want to taste *kajmak*![10] Valentina's even started nagging me that I cook food that is too greasy and complains about the dishes that I've been preparing for forty years now! And she won't eat my cakes anymore because they have too much butter and walnuts and they are overly 'heavy' for her!"

In the view of mothers, such a change was never only a change in taste—it implied a change of heart too. Gorica handwrote a cookbook with recipes she had collected throughout her life and gifted it to her daughter so she would not forget the recipes from her mother and the place where she had grown up. Gorica regretfully noted that Valentina mainly used that cookbook to surprise her foreign friends. "Mostly, though," explained Gorica, "she prepared different food, like meat with oranges or fish with coconut milk. Her husband lived in Asia for a while, and Valentina cooks dishes that he learned to love there. They are delicious, but they are very different from the tastes we are used to."

While this repudiation of mothers' food occurred in both men and women migrants, the reasons were interpreted differently. When a son rejected his mother's food and cooking, the mother considered it to be the daughter-in-law's influence. Had it not been for the daughter-in-law, the mother's reasoning went, her son would have still loved his mother's cooking. Mothers struggled more to understand why their daughters had rejected their recipes and way of cooking. Migrant daughters saw this as a natural process of distancing themselves from their mothers and finding their own identity as women. To cut the umbilical cord connecting them to their mothers, migrant women repudiated both the food and recipes that their mothers sent them. As Nina, one of my London informants—a single woman in her late thirties back in 2005—commented: "I don't want to be a slave to the family and to spend all my free time tied to the cooker like my mother. Our dishes take ages to prepare, and they are full of grease and *zaprška* [a thickening sauce made of oil, flour, and paprika]. I am not a child any longer—I know what is good for me, and such food certainly isn't! I stopped drinking coffee and switched to green tea instead, I eat fresh vegetables and fruit as much as possible, and I'd much rather eat sushi, pasta, and salads than *sarma* and *gibanica*."[11]

The examples of Radoslava, Gorica, and Nina illustrate how this change in diet and cooking has an entirely different meaning for mothers and their children. While mothers considered the transformation in their adult children's taste and food preferences to be a repudiation of themselves, their cooking, and tradition, children justified their choice as proof of their maturity and ability to decide what was right and healthy. What mothers viewed as a rejection symbolized freedom of choice and a sign of maturity for adult children. For Nina, adopting her mother's recipes and cooking meant "becoming" her mother, assuming the role of a self-sacrificing woman that she, living far from Serbia and its societal norms and expectations, felt free to reject. She was not rejecting her mother, per se, but a memory that her mother's cooking evoked.

That very memory for a mother is what Annette Weiner terms "inalienable possessions"—an implicit knowledge passed on from one generation to another.[12] A mother's inability to fulfill her mission of cultural transmission of such possessions calls into question the very identity of a mother as an elderly matriarch in a society. It is more evident in the cases here how vital food—in particular, cooked food—is for instilling the memory of one's family, ancestors, origin, and home (in a material sense).

Gorica's case was typical of many Belgrade mothers of migrant sons and daughters. Similarly to Radoslava, Gorica struggled to instill the memory of home through food in different ways: cooking for her daughter and her family when they came to visit, bringing them food from Serbia when she visited them, and sending them food. The most important of these seemed to be the process of preparing food: doing things the same way as one's mother and grandmother had done created a connection between generations and affirmed one's belonging to a particular family. Because it involved a specific method of preparation usually attached to one's mother's way of cooking, cooked food was also much more contested, especially among migrant women who used cooking as a way of distancing themselves from their mothers to a greater or lesser degree. This coming of age was much more dramatic in young women because their mothers expected them to be the bearers of family traditions and partake in the process of cultural transmission. Much less pressure was put on men, and even when they tried to distance themselves from their mothers' influence, this was usually interpreted as the fault of their wives or partners, as we see in Radoslava's case. Cooked food in the context of migration becomes a battlefield where several armies clash with each other: family tradition, mother-daughter relationship, partner relationship, one's place of origin, and a relationship with an adopted foreign culture.

However, just because post-Yugoslav migrants had lost interest in traditionally cooked Serbian food, this did not mean they rejected all food from Serbia. Raw, uncooked food was one such exception. Most kinds of fruit and vegetables in Belgrade at the time of my fieldwork in the mid-2000s were still available, mainly during their specific seasons. They were sold mostly in open food markets, seldom in supermarkets.[13] During my 2006 fieldwork in Belgrade, cherries and strawberries were in season. On a regular shopping trip to a food market, Gorica was pleasantly surprised to find large, dark red, sweet and juicy cherries—they were her daughter's favorites. Later that day, when she spoke to Valentina on the phone, Gorica told her about the *rompavice*, as she called this type of cherry. Valentina responded that she had been thinking about them just the other day; it had been years since she had had them, and she asked Gorica to bring cherries next time she visited because they reminded her of childhood. Such raw food, carrying a memory of childhood, seemed unproblematic compared to cooked food, which had the power to re-create the present because it involved accepting a set of coded cooking practices instilled by one's ancestors.[14]

Brand-name, cooked, and raw food all evoked different memories. Brand-name food conjured up historical and social memories of Yugoslavia, raw food such as fruits and vegetables triggered personal memories from childhood, and cooked food summoned memories of one's family and one's mother or grandmother—her way of doing things and her cooking. Cooked food was intensely ethnically marked. There were stark differences in cooking between Vojvodina (the northern province), Central Serbia, Slavonia in Croatia, Bosnia-Herzegovina, and Montenegro. Belgrade mothers brought into their homes their inherited way of cooking, as they had learned it from their mothers or from their mothers-in-law to please their husbands, and passed on this ethnic and regional heritage to their daughters and sons.

In the case of post-Yugoslav migrants from Belgrade, food and cooking triggered memories on several levels and in some instances prompted the process of structured forgetting. It was not uncommon that some of the post-Yugoslav migrants wanted to forget some parts of their identity. Cooked food was much more potent than raw or brand-name food in reminding one where he or she came from: not only did it bring out personal memories, as food brands from Yugoslavia did, but also memories of one's lineage and ethnic background. In the case of economic migrants or migrants from earlier, politically motivated migration waves, this would probably not be the case. But for migrants coming from a country destroyed by ethnic conflict, cooked food became a highly contested memory that many of those fleeing the war wanted to forget and leave behind.[15]

Similarly to Radoslava's son, the only things that Valentina still asked her mother, Gorica, to bring her were books—novels for herself and children's books and songs for her toddler son to help him learn Serbian. This was the case at the time of my fieldwork in 2006. Gorica noted that in the first few years after she had emigrated, Valentina was still interested in reading newspapers and magazines and keeping up to date with new actors, singers, and cultural events in Serbia. As time went by, Gorica remarked ruefully, her daughter lost interest in gossip magazines and only wanted *Politikin Zabavnik*,[16] a weekly magazine that she started reading when she was five. There is a parallel between this example and the previous one involving cherries. In both instances, there is an apparent wish on Valentina's part to evoke memories from childhood and repudiate the coevalness her mother tried to create:[17] for Valentina, the taste of home her mother brought was a taste of her childhood home, whereas for Gorica, the taste of home she wanted to deliver to her daughter was that of her current homeland. Had Valentina not emigrated but stayed in Belgrade, her mother would not have had to recreate this sense of "home" because Valentina would have had space for negotiating her experience of home.

As Gorica noted, not only had there been a change in her daughter's interest in Serbian food and local show business news compared to the early days of emigration, but Valentina's gifts to her were reduced to a box of chocolates. As soon as she noted this, Gorica hastened to add that it was not that she needed anything. "I am old," explained Gorica, "and if I need something, I can buy it at the Chinese market."[18]

Reminiscing about the gifts that Valentina had brought her in the past, Gorica proudly showed a coffee set displayed in a glass cabinet. It was a bit surprising to find such a practical gift stored away like a museum exhibit. Gorica conceded that her daughter had wanted her parents to use the set so that they would think of Valentina when they drank coffee. Gorica, however, was afraid that the set might break with everyday use and decided to store it instead. Gorica also mentioned that in the past, Valentina used to buy her perfume. Valentina would buy her mother the same fragrance she purchased for herself because she wanted her to be trendy. However, instead of using those perfumes, her mother was keeping them intact for her daughter to use while in Belgrade. She proudly showed me the perfume bottles she had received from her daughter over the last fourteen years, remarking that she kept the bottles and could not throw them away even though they were empty. She concluded:

> She used to bring more things before, but this has changed; it faded away . . . maybe because everything is different in Belgium than in Portugal. We don't understand each other so well like before. She doesn't understand me and thinks I try too hard to please everyone in the family, that I am too much concerned with respecting certain formalities [in kin relationships]. Probably

because there, in Belgium, they live differently. We are a big family—five brothers and sisters. We all live in different towns, but we speak at least once a week on the phone. Sometimes we even text each other. Last week, for instance, I was away on vacation, and I sent a text message to my sister for her birthday. Valentina thinks that's too much. Time has taken its toll; she has changed. I can't say it's the same like it was in the past. She's been away from the country since 1992. And that is a long time.

Gorica's insistence on how her relationship to her daughter changed after she moved from Portugal to Belgium is noteworthy. Even though Gorica did not emphasize this, while in Portugal, her daughter was not married and had no children. Valentina moved to Belgium because her husband was Belgian and they decided to start a family there. One could argue that the change Gorica described in her relationship with her daughter had more to do with her daughter's change of marital status and the fact that she had become a mother herself, than—as Gorica claimed—with a change of country. While living in Portugal, Valentina had a boyfriend from Serbia, and most of her friends there were from the former Yugoslavia. Upon migration from Portugal to a small town in Belgium, she found herself married to a foreign husband, with a baby, and without a job or the friends from Serbia she had had in Portugal. Gorica's reaction to her daughter's decision to move to Belgium was a bit too exaggerated for her concern to have been only about a new country. Gorica reflected on this event: "She had such a beautiful apartment on the coast, a bit further from Lisbon, very similar to our Opatija, but she decided to leave it and to move to Belgium with her husband.[19] She tried to comfort me and said she would find a job in Belgium. I got an overactive thyroid worrying whether she would find a job and how she would manage in a new country, starting from scratch again. In the end it all worked out, but it was all touch and go in the beginning."

Valentina had migrated for the second time because her partner was living in Belgium and she wanted to start a family with him. The daughter's founding of her family household and subsequent experience of motherhood represented the most significant change in this mother-daughter relationship. Changing country was merely a consequence of a life-cycle transformation in which a daughter became a wife and mother. The difference in Valentina's cooking following her marriage to a foreign husband, her rejection of her mother's "greasy" and "unhealthy" recipes, and her embrace of different cuisines that her husband preferred—these were not just a consequence of her moving from Portugal to Belgium but instead indicated her shifting within a life-cycle and changing her relationship to her mother. In other words, Valentina repudiated the normative expectations of her mother, simultaneously creating her own norms in her relationship with her child.

Ljubica emigrated from Belgrade to London in the early 1990s.[20] At the time, Ljubica was engaged to an Englishman who lived in Belgrade. When the UN imposed sanctions on Serbia, Ljubica and her fiancé, David, decided to move to England. Several years after they moved to the United Kingdom, Ljubica's parents came to visit them. They brought a suitcase full of homemade food delicacies: *ajvar* that one of Ljubica's aunts had prepared, *slatko* (fruit preserves) her mother had made, goat cheese from her aunt in Montenegro, and *pršuta* (smoked air-dried ham) from another aunt in Montenegro. Even frozen trout arrived in the suitcase because her mother considered it to be better than the trout in the United Kingdom. Ljubica was profoundly touched when she saw the abundance of food and the effort that her whole family had made to send it. With each visit, her parents brought other presents that they thought she would like and need. Gifts included a set of Zepter pots and pans; tablecloths; crocheted items; and Ljubica's books, photographs, and childhood photo albums.[21] Ljubica became slightly apologetic when she showed me the tablecloths and crochet work made by her relatives that she had received as gifts from her mother. They were old-fashioned, and Ljubica was unlikely to cover her cabinets and tables with them. Not wanting to part with them, however, Ljubica kept them neatly tucked away in a kitchen cupboard—close enough to remind her they were there but out of sight so as not to interfere with her taste in home furnishings.

A common theme throughout these cases is the relationship between memory and kinship. We mostly see mothers' efforts to instill certain memories in their children and grandchildren through food. In these cases, eating food from one's homeland was the closest one could get to "tasting home." Food in the context of nostalgia for home has been a subject of some excellent anthropological studies.[22] However, in this particular case, we see how grandparents use food as a medium for conveying a specific kind of memory, not necessarily of themselves as individuals but of the extended family to which their children and grandchildren belonged, as well as memories of the tradition and culture of their ancestors. We see in Ljubica's case that sending food can involve efforts by aunts and other relatives not only from Belgrade but also from distant and different regions of the former Yugoslavia. Certainly, Ljubica's aunts did not doubt that she could find trout, white cheese, and *ajvar* in London—of course she could. But those were not the trout, white cheese, or *ajvar* in which they had invested their time and effort to source ingredients, prepare, and deliver to her. It was not just any *ajvar*; it had been homemade by her aunt, who spent hours roasting red peppers in the boiling summer heat, then peeling them, grinding them, cooking them, and finally filling jars with the mixture and storing it for the winter. And that is just the beginning of the story of the *ajvar*, which then traveled from Montenegro to Serbia. From Belgrade, Ljubica's mother had to smuggle it through to London, get safely past the customs officers, and finally present it to Ljubica. The whole point of sending this jar of *ajvar* to Ljubica was not because she was that fond of it or because this was what she liked to eat when she was a child. The point of the endeavor was to remind her of a whole network of relatives whose sacrifices attested to their position vis-à-vis her, as well as to her position within the kin network. Thus we see how the work of memory constitutes kinship and how gifting practices are used in the context of migration to affirm one's place in a kinship group.

Furthermore, by passing on their ways of preparing food and by sharing the knowledge and experience inherited from their female ancestors—as Weiner's "inalienable possessions"—mothers also affirmed their power and authority over their daughters and their family.[23] This was of vital importance in a patriarchal and male-dominated society like Serbia's, in which women's sphere of domination is reduced to domesticity and family. The elderly Belgrade mothers are by no means an exclusive example when it comes to food, self-sacrifice, and power. Carole Counihan argues that Florentine women's identity is "other-directed" and that "the older women believe they should struggle to prevent pain for others, even at the cost of absorbing it themselves."[24] One of the critical insights in Counihan's work is that, similarly to Belgrade mothers, Italian mothers used food and cooking to gain power, and through this process, they acted as transmitters of culture.[25]

The notable difference, however, between Belgrade and Florentine mothers is that, following the collapse of Yugoslavia and the massive outmigration of young adults, elderly Belgrade mothers lost one of their only sources of power in a patriarchal Serbian society. With no one to look after, to cook for, and to sacrifice for, these mothers lost a considerable part of themselves, as well as the power they had before their children's emigration. Thus, sending homemade food and instilling their way of cooking in their migrant daughters became vital elements of preserving their identity as mothers in a chaotic post-socialist Serbian society. Mothers knew full well that their daughters would not starve abroad. This was not why they were so concerned about the transmission of recipes for homemade meals. Through this food-related work—writing down recipes for their daughters, cooking, and sending food abroad—women "did" their gender and affirmed their identity as mothers, precariously threatened by brutal reality as their families—and their familiar worlds—unraveled.

Notes

Some sections of this chapter appear in "Food, Family, and Memory: Belgrade Mothers and Their Migrant Children," *Food and Foodways: Explorations in the History and Culture of Human Nourishment* 21, no. 1 (2013), 46–65.

1. Sutton, *Remembrance of Repasts.*
2. For studies about the significance of food for migrants, see Lee, "Dys-appearing Tongues"; Mankekar, "'India Shopping'"; Ray, *The Migrant's Table*; Roden, *Book of Middle Eastern Food*; Roy, "Reading Communities"; and Sutton, *Remembrance of Repasts.*
3. Radoslava, interview by author, Belgrade, May 11, 2006.
4. "*Daleko od očiju, daleko od srca.*"
5. Proust, *In Search of Lost Time.*
6. Compare this to the case of elderly Korean migrants in Japan whose stomachs have, after many years spent in Japan, become sensitive to spicy Korean food, which they interpret as their moral failure in not remaining sufficiently Korean (Lee, "Dys-appearing Tongues," 202–3, cited in Holtzman, "Food and Memory," 367).
7. DeVault, *Feeding the Family*, 39.
8. Ibid., 48.
9. Gorica, interview by author, Belgrade, May 11, 2006.
10. *Kajmak* is a dairy product made from the fat skimmed off cooked milk and left to ferment. It is salty and has a high fat content of about 60 percent. Dairy farmers make and sell *kajmak* in farmers' markets, not in grocery stores.
11. Nina, interview by author, London, February 11. 2006. *Sarma* is made out of pickled cabbage leaves stuffed with mince meat and rice and cooked on low heat for several hours. *Gibanica* is a type of savory pie made of layers of filo pastry and white cow cheese mixed with eggs.
12. Weiner, *Inalienable Possessions.* See also Munn, *The Fame of Gawa.*
13. Although fresh fruits and vegetables could be found in supermarkets, they were more expensive and of worse quality. Only a few years later, however, because of changes in food distribution channels in Serbia, fruit and vegetables have now become available year-round in supermarkets at lower prices.
14. For comparison with food's ability to inspire personal memories in rural Greece, see Seremetakis, "The Memory of the Senses"; see also Sutton, *Remembrance of Repasts.*
15. For comparison, see Bock-Luna, *The Past in Exile.*
16. *Politikin Zabavnik* is a weekly magazine with a mixture of educational and funny content. Advertised as a magazine for people aged 7 to 107, it is not uncommon to find grown-ups reading it.

17. See Fabian, *Time and the Other*.

18. The Chinese market was much cheaper than main street shops in Belgrade. Many of my informants lamented that they felt let down by the post-socialist clothing market. Familiar Yugoslav socialist clothing brands had disappeared, and Zara, H&M, and other Western brands that arrived in the post-socialist period, complained my informants, sold inappropriate and overpriced clothes for women of their age. The socialist clothing brands they trusted used superior-quality natural fabrics like cotton, wool, and silk, unlike the trendy, expensive Western brands that used synthetic textiles of much lower quality. The Chinese market was far from ideal, I was told, but it filled a gap in the women's clothing market, offering inexpensive clothes that women could afford with their pensions.

19. Opatija is a small tourist town near the seaport of Rijeka on the northern Croatian coastline. It is interesting to note the use of "our" here. For many people of Gorica's generation, who had lived in Yugoslavia for most of their lives, many places that are now part of Croatia, Macedonia, Slovenia, Bosnia-Herzegovina, or Montenegro are still referred to as "ours," especially when juxtaposed with other foreign places. In other words, even though they are not part of Serbia, they are still more recognizably "theirs" than any other foreign place.

20. Ljubica, interview by author, London, November 16, 2005.

21. Women in 1990s Serbia greatly valued Zepter cooking sets. They were thought to promote healthier cooking. They were also very expensive, and people often paid for them in twenty-four-month installments.

22. See Seremetakis, "The Memory of the Senses"; Duruz, "Food as Nostalgia"; Petridou, "The Taste of Home"; Sutton, *Remembrance of Repasts*; Mankekar, "'India Shopping'"; Roy, "Reading Communities"; and Counihan, *Around the Tuscan Table*.

23. Weiner, *Inalienable Possessions*.

24. Counihan, *The Anthropology of Food*, 52.

25. See Counihan, *The Anthropology of Food*, "Food as Woman's Voice," and *Around the Tuscan Table*.

3

WEAVING THE ORDER

Homes and Everyday Practices of Belgrade Mothers

I SPENT MOST OF MY BELGRADE FIELDWORK IN the homes of parents. With one or two exceptions, I always met my research participants in their homes in Belgrade.[1] Their daily routines consisted of a short walk to the newsstand, to a local grocery shop or nearby farmers' market, or to visit the doctor or a neighbor. For elderly mothers, the home was where they spent most, if not all, of their time. The majority of their socializing with friends and neighbors happened at home. The home was also a physical embodiment of their relationship with their children.

The material culture of the home reveals more about the relationship between mothers and their migrant children than any conversation or interview ever could. Embodied practices and engagement with the material world of home provide the perfect avenue for understanding the construction of gender through doing.[2] Likewise, mothers' engagement with everyday household routines highlights that a family is also socially constructed. A family "is not a naturally occurring collection of individuals," according to Marjorie DeVault, rather "its reality is constructed from day to day through activities like eating together."[3] What happens, then, when children leave home, often without returning to visit, and mothers remain on their own? If a family is constructed through doing things together, this implies that for an elderly woman living alone there is no mother and no family left. Yet this chapter suggests that women were not ready to surrender their motherhood without a fight. The women went to extremes to preserve their identity as mothers both for themselves and their families. They re-created everyday rituals, substituting objects in place of children and families that represented them or reminded the mother of her children.

By doing so, they had something as mothers to hold on to, something to give them a sense of direction and purpose.

The study of the material culture of home and embodied practices also highlights the asymmetry inherent in the mother-child relationship. Despite a palpable sense of pride in their migrant children, an unsettling sorrow underlies these mothers' narratives. The way they talked about children who had left ten or fifteen years ago gives the impression that they were talking about someone who had passed away, someone no longer present in their lives. In many cases, mothers remembered the exact date and circumstances of their son's or daughter's departure, as we see with Gorica in chapter 2.[4] In contrast, very few of my London research participants remembered the exact date they had left Belgrade. However, this atmosphere of mourning, which pervaded almost all of my Belgrade fieldwork, was specific in the sense that the "departed" were not dead. Their children's absence was very much present and was materially manifested—from the way mothers preserved their children's rooms, what they did with their photographs, and how they continued to cook for their children and celebrate their birthdays in absentia to the way they structured their time, daily routines, and activities around their children's lives.

Retired mothers whose children lived abroad often organized their daily routines around their migrant children's time zone and activities. They knew when their children were at work, when they were at home, when they went to sleep, and when was the best time to talk to them. In mothers' homes, I often came across a clock showing the time in New York, Toronto, or Sydney—places where their children lived. The division of space within parents' homes was different compared to the homes of migrants in London. Migrants' homes told stories of their new lives, of their class and social aspirations in their new country. These homes reflected an effort at finding a thread between one's childhood and youth in Yugoslavia, one's journey through immigration and perhaps seeking asylum, and one's social aspirations in a new city and new country. Sometimes they contained childhood memories associated with the town they grew up in and with popular culture such as music and films from those times. With a single exception, there were no signs of parents' presence in the homes of migrants I worked with in London.[5] Any gifts from mothers were carefully stored away, out of sight but at hand if and when needed.

Mothers' homes told a very different story. Their homes were troves of family memories. Nothing was displayed without reason. These were mothers' attempts at chronicling their family's history, their children's growing up, and the times spent together within those four walls. As much as these homes were devoid of people who had once inhabited them, their absence was carefully furnished—paradoxically, very much present—through embodiment in mothers' practices. The care with which mothers kept any gift they received from their migrant children was truly poignant. As we have already witnessed in the previous chapter, a coffee set from one's daughter was not to be used on a daily basis but was carefully exhibited in a display cabinet. Even empty perfume bottles were kept as memories of a migrant daughter who had brought them as presents for her mother.

This chapter presents several homes, describing how mothers organized their time and space once their children had emigrated abroad. Although there are many differences between these particular cases, they also share specific common themes. Regardless of the quality of the relationship between mothers and children, this connection is deeply rooted in home and things that constituted home.

Curator of the Family Museum

Milena was a retired woman in her mid-sixties who lived alone in a four-bedroom apartment in Vidikovac, on the outskirts of Belgrade.[6] Her son and daughter had moved to New York City in 1993. They both went on tourist visas to visit a relative and, as the situation in Belgrade worsened, they extended their stay. The son had not been back to Belgrade since; he was afraid the army would arrest him and prevent him from leaving Serbia because he had not done his compulsory military service.[7] The daughter had visited Serbia once to have cancer surgery that she could not afford in the United States.

As I entered Milena's apartment, I noticed numerous photographs all around. Milena described herself as a strict mother, realistic and critical toward her children. When the children had left home, though, she let her emotions overcome her. "If I have to open a photo album each time I want to see them, it is too complicated," explained Milena. So she taped photocopied photographs of her children and grandchildren on the walls, on top of the wallpaper. "This way they are always around me wherever I move around the home."

Milena wanted to move out of the apartment, both because it was too big and expensive to maintain on her pension and because she did not like the area. It reminded her of the NATO bombing in 1999, during which that part of the city sustained massive hits. However, she said, "This apartment is full of memories of my children, and I can't leave them." Every day for Milena started with a ritual. She got up, went to her son's room to look at his photos on the walls, went out to the balcony to see what the weather was like outside, then left the balcony through her daughter's room, kissed her grandchildren's photos in her daughter's room, and returned to her son's room to check whether there was an email waiting from one of them. She took me around the home to demonstrate the itinerary of her ritual. I was surprised that posters of Blondie, Duran Duran, and other bands from the 1980s still hung on the walls in her son's room. Milena explained that she had tried to keep the room as it was when her son left because she wanted it to have his mark. The only changes she made were putting a computer on her son's desk and covering the walls with her son's photographs. She pointed at the photographs on the walls, explaining:

> Now and then I hear someone saying, 'Oh, you're lucky, your children are in America.' And I say, 'Yes, I am happy. And I wish that yours will be there as well if they aren't already.' And then my throat gets stiff and I think to myself, 'Then you would see what the sorrow is.' My heart is full, but my eyes are empty. I would like them [gesturing at her grandchildren in a photo] to rush into the house right now, and I would like to be able to say, 'Oh, here they are!' All this [pointing at photos on the walls] is hollow. You know the Jewish saying, 'May you have all and then lose everything'—well, this is it.

Milena was undoubtedly happy that her son did not go to war and that both he and her daughter had found better opportunities overseas. However, the emptiness left in their wake was palpable. Instead of finding comfort from the people around her, Milena encountered envy. I asked Milena if she had neighbors or friends living nearby with whom she could chat over coffee:

> I don't like socializing with neighbors because they are resentful that my children are abroad and don't suffer like their children here. I would rather die than tell them how I really feel: how the emptiness hurts, and how long months and years can be when you sit here on your own and wait. I sit here [pointing to the living room] or in my son's room, play video games, search for e-cards on the internet for my grandson, and wait. . . . [pause] I wait for their email, text message, anything. And secretly I hope that one day they will surprise me and burst through the door.

To ease the pain, Milena holds onto objects reminiscent of her children and grandchildren abroad, breathing life into them through daily rituals around her home. As I followed Milena's routine around the apartment, I noticed some objects that seemed to be randomly placed here and there—small seashells, pebbles, an awkwardly shaped vase, a green plate hanging on a wall—and between them, numerous photographs of her grandchildren in America. Milena explained that each object was a memory of someone or some event. Her four-year-old grandson had collected the seashells and given them to her. The pebbles came from her son; the vase she had received as a wedding gift from her maid of honor almost forty years ago; the plate was a gift from her sister who lived in Sweden, and so on. She explained these were all memories that she could not throw away: "Each of them reminds me of someone I love or of some precious moment in life. They keep me company now that everybody has left the house. My sister and my mother have been living in Sweden for almost thirty years; my children have been in New York for more than ten years. I am divorced, and my ex-husband lives in another town."

Milena's case poignantly illustrates the difficulties of adapting to life-changing events such as divorce and the migration of adult children. Things in her apartment, abandoned by her ex-husband and children, reminded her of the life that had once taken place in her household. They provided material evidence of a past life that she struggled to let go. Milena decided to stay in that apartment, although she did not like its location and found it too big and the upkeep too expensive.[8] In many respects, Milena seemed both a guardian and a prisoner of this museum—while she painstakingly preserved the artifacts that embodied her relationship with her children and their relationship to her as a mother, her frustration at her inability to leave the apartment was quite noticeable. Not only was the apartment a financial burden she could not shoulder with her pension, but it was also a painful reminder of the family that had once lived in it. Being alone in this space only exacerbated her loneliness and feeling of abandonment, yet she could not bring herself to leave this poignant museum.

Photographs are very particular objects because they are created in an attempt to capture the present moment, to freeze it and preserve it for the future as a memory.[9] Writing about photographs and memory, Elizabeth Edwards notes that "photographs impose themselves on memory. They become surrogate memory and their silences structure forgetting."[10] Children remain children in photographs, just as mothers remain mothers, even when the reality may have changed. Photographs airbrush some memories and immortalize those depicted in them. A child pictured in a photo will always remain that same child. The image does not capture the changing nature of a mother-child relationship but reflects one particular moment in that relationship. This echoes John Berger's idea of a photograph, that "it isolates, preserves and presents a moment taken from a continuum."[11] The ritual that Milena performed every morning—greeting her children and grandchildren depicted in photographs, walking through rooms preserved as they were when her children left many years ago—affirmed her role of mother and grandmother.

This ritual also created a sense of order and stability in her ever-changing reality. Even though Milena divorced her husband because he struggled with alcoholism, she nevertheless mourned their family life because there had been someone to share the everydayness with. Within the space of a few years, she was all alone: both children were in the United States, and her ex-husband relocated to a different town. After years of living in a full house, she was suddenly on her own and struggling to come to terms with those unsettling changes. Her friends and neighbors had little sympathy for her; with two children living abroad who were able, in their view, to support her financially, they considered her to be in a better position than themselves. They did not seem to notice Milena's suffering—she just could not get used to being so alone and so far away from everyone she cared about and loved. Her mother and sister were migrants as well, having lived in Sweden for several decades. All she could do was remind herself every morning of the mother and grandmother she was to her migrant children and grandchildren, kiss their photos, and then face the world alone.

The importance of photographs and of preserving migrants' possessions intact, resembling mourning rituals for the deceased, has been beautifully portrayed by novelist Orhan Pamuk. Writing about his grandmother's home, the Turkish Nobel laureate notes, "There, in the library, gathering dust behind the glass, were my doctor uncle's medical books: in the twenty years since he'd emigrated to America, no human hand had touched them. To my childish mind, these rooms were furnished not for the living but for the dead."[12] As he continues to describe photographs in his grandmother's living room, Pamuk stops at a photo of the migrant uncle—the uncle "who went to America to study medicine without first doing his military service and so was never able to return to Turkey, thus paving the way for my grandmother to spend the rest of her life assuming mournful airs."[13]

It is this impossibility of return—whether because of conscription, war, or unresolved legal status in one's host country—that creates an atmosphere of mothers' mourning for migrant children. If it were not for the efforts of their mothers, these migrant children would be socially dead (within their extended families) in the land of their births—thus, the necessity of keeping their photographs in the most prominent place within the household, of keeping their gifts visible to all visitors, of creating the impression of their physical presence in their mothers' homes. Through these rituals of mourning, mothers maintain the presence of their absent children. Following the logic of DeVault's argument about family and mothers coming into reality through practice, there is no family—and ultimately, no mother—without these daily rituals and activities performed within the intimacy of home.[14]

Weaving the Order

Unlike Milena, Mirjana had no photos or other visible memories of her son or his family on display in her home.[15] Her son had moved to Canada as an economic migrant because he could not find a job with his university degree in Belgrade. He had been living in Toronto for sixteen years at the time of my fieldwork. By then he held a stable job and had bought a house and settled down. He was married and had two teenage daughters, both of whom had been born in Canada.

As I entered the apartment, Mirjana showed me into a small living room connected to an open kitchen. There were three chairs in the room, and I was not sure where to sit; I asked her which was her chair, as I did not want to impose. "Oh, you will impose wherever you sit—they are all my chairs," replied Mirjana, not mincing her words. Her curt answer and strict attitude matched the immaculate order and tidiness of her home. I asked Mirjana whether she had pictures of her granddaughters, and she replied matter-of-factly: "I like children in general, but I don't feel my son's daughters like my [blood]. They are not growing up next to me; I am not used to them. He [the son] doesn't send their photos, I am not asking for them, and I don't participate in their lives. As if they don't exist."

Mirjana's reaction was quite unusual, as most mothers and even the few fathers that featured in my research seemed on average more eager to talk about their grandchildren. I then asked if she had any photos of her son, and she replied with unreserved bitterness in her tone: "No, why would I keep his photos? He is the same. We stayed the same, my son and me. He still likes to get on my nerves like when he was a boy. I was angry with him for leaving me like that; I didn't speak to him for two years after he'd gone away. My husband died just before my son left, and I was left all alone and with no income. I know that he had a difficult time there [in Canada], but I didn't want to know—it was his choice to leave."

More than fifteen years following her son's departure, Mirjana still seemed upset, and she did not try to hide it. After her husband's death, Mirjana expected her son to stay nearby. Instead, he left for Canada, leaving his mother to face the onslaught of the 1990s alone with her modest pension. Her home spoke to her restrained anger but also to her tremendous effort in putting order into life and creating new meaning in what was a hard time for her.

While *gobleni*—needlepoint replicas of the famous Gobelin tapestries— adorned the walls of many homes I visited in Belgrade, Mirjana's home stood out because her tapestries covered virtually every wall. Mirjana proudly explained that she had made every single one. The tapestries were arranged according to the purpose of the room: in the living room, she had hung a tapestry of Leonardo Da Vinci's *The Last Supper* that covered the central part of one wall. Mirjana stressed that it had taken her eighteen months to complete that tapestry, recounting the difficult events that had happened in her life during the period of its creation. The tapestry was material evidence, a medal reminding her of a battlefield. As we proceeded from room to room, it turned out that needlepoint had always been a retreat for her, enabling her to devote time to herself and divert her thoughts away from her problems.

Varying styles of frames hinted at the different periods when these tapestries were created. Some of the tapestries had been hanging there for thirty or forty years; Mirjana could not find the same style frames anymore. She showed me the most recent two, each portraying a little girl, and explained: "This is my family. They keep me company here day after day. I see them grow before my eyes. I am currently doing a tapestry with a picture of a fawn so that 'my girls' have someone to play with." I asked her if she planned to give some of the tapestries to her son, as there was barely any space left on the walls to hang them, and she replied, "Every time I ask him or his family if they want any of my tapestries, they refuse. I will offer these new tapestries with a girl to my granddaughters, but I don't expect they would be interested in them."

While showing me the tapestries hanging throughout her apartment, Mirjana explained how she had redistributed the space since living on her own. To the left of the entrance, there was a bedroom that had belonged to her and her late husband and where, since her husband's death, she had been living on her own. There were several smaller tapestries in that room, mostly depicting children. Right next to the bedroom, there was a smaller box room that used to be her son's room before he immigrated to Canada. Mirjana had turned this into her "workroom" for her tapestries. She proudly showed me the room, adding, "This is where I spend most of my time and create my family day after day," as she pointed to an unfinished tapestry that, together with threads and needles, was resting on the bed. A long hallway connected that part of the apartment to a small open-plan kitchen and a living room. Tapestries covered the wall in the corridor as well; these were smaller to fit the space.[16] Those in the living room were also smaller and were mostly landscapes, whereas the most impressive ones, like *The Last Supper*, were hanging in the living room.

For each tapestry, Mirjana knew exactly how old she had been when she made it and what she had been going through in life—pregnancy, her baby, her husband's death, her son's departure, and so on. When I remarked how strenuous it must have been to spend all those hours doing thousands of stitches and making such elaborate tapestries, Mirjana abruptly added that this was never tiring. Moreover, she rushed to add, it was only then that she could relax and divert her thoughts away from the difficulties she was experiencing. Tapestries marked dramatic events in Mirjana's life and gave her comfort and a sense of stability that she was creating herself. She took pride in having good eyesight and a steady hand that enabled her to continue to make tapestries in her late sixties.

Each stitch in the tapestry was a memory woven into the tangible fabric of life. All the things that she could not change in life—her husband's death and the financial hardship that followed, her only child's departure from the country and her subsequent sense of (both emotional and financial) abandonment, a feeling of detachment from her granddaughters who were growing up far away—were sewn, stitch after stitch, into her tapestries. The stitches, however, not only marked loss but created new meanings as well. The tapestries that depicted little girls, and another one with a fawn who was to be "a friend" for "her girls," was a family that Mirjana created for herself—granddaughters that she could grow with her hands. Stitching seemed to empower Mirjana not only to create order in the turbulent and difficult periods in her life but to give life to her own family—the two granddaughters that she raised stitch after stitch, by her side all the time.

She looked after them, they had their room, and she was even making them a friend so that they could play together.

Similarly to Milena, Mirjana went from living in a family to being all alone very quickly. In a post-socialist and postconflict society where nothing seemed stable or recognizable, such substantial changes to one's circumstances posed considerable challenges. Mirjana's way of coping with so many profound changes was to create her world with needle and thread, one that she could be responsible for and look after. Even when she had a family to tend, it seemed that no matter what happened during the day, Mirjana would never be too tired for needlework in the evening. Each stitch was a sigh of relief. This case was not an exception. In her ethnographic work about weavers in southern Morocco, Myriem Naji notes how women often described the engrossing effect of working on motifs that made them forget their worries and problems.[17] Women created agency through submitting to technical and social self-constraints.[18] Technology and aesthetics, Naji argues, "cannot be separated from emotions, ethics and the gendering of subjects."[19] Despite the apparent differences between Moroccan society and Serbian post-socialist society, the process of creating agency, expressing emotions, and finding solace in needlepoint or weaving is a common thread. In the disorienting everyday experience of the 1990s, further exacerbated by changes in personal circumstances such as divorce, a partner's death, and children's emigration, creating agency and order became paramount to one's survival. Some were creating this order through everyday rituals around their homes, reminding themselves of the space once inhabited by children no longer there. Others, like Mirjana, were creating order and agency through their practice of stitching.

The Mother of a Child, Past and Present

Tapestries played an essential role in another household I visited. Ana was a widowed mother whose only son had emigrated to Australia ten years earlier with his wife and two children, leaving his elderly mother behind.[20] Ana's son was a mechanical engineer, his wife was an architect, and they had not been able to secure a living with their degrees in Serbia in the 1990s. Ana's daughter-in-law struggled to find work in the mid-1990s, as most construction projects in Serbia had ground to a halt because of the war and the UN sanctions. She would go to the office and do some work, but the company was not paying her. Ana's son had to volunteer and hope that someday he might be offered a job. He, his wife, and their two children had shared a one-bedroom apartment with Ana and her husband, as they could not afford to live independently. Ana and her husband moved to the living room and gave the couple their bedroom, where they squeezed in with their two children. While such living arrangements were not unusual in Belgrade and in Serbia more generally at the time, they were nevertheless difficult for most to get used to and quite often served as a catalyst for people considering emigration. As a highly skilled couple with university degrees in engineering and architecture, living in one bedroom with two children and with his elderly parents living in the living room of the same tiny apartment, Ana's son and daughter-in-law were a typical example of the Serbian brain drain migration in the 1990s. Their university degrees and skills were useless in the country under the UN embargo, which brought industry to a standstill, and where the only job opportunities lay in smuggling. In the 1990s, Australia, New Zealand, and Canada had a points-based system that allowed highly skilled migrants to apply for settlement visas. Thousands of young, highly skilled men and women emigrated from Serbia to these three countries during the last decade of the previous century. Sons of Ana, Mirjana, and Radoslava were among these young men who emigrated to Canada and Australia as highly skilled migrants. The military draft provided an additional push factor that propelled these men into deciding to emigrate at any cost, including leaving their elderly mothers on their own. They were not only saving their lives from the war in which they did not want to participate but securing for themselves a more prosperous future.

Ana had a minuscule stocking repair shop and worked continuously for almost sixty years.[21] Even though she was nearly eighty at the time of my fieldwork in 2006, she still occasionally took an order from an old customer. Like Mirjana, she had also been creating tapestries throughout her life. Each tapestry represented a memory of a significant event. Ana explained her passion for needlepoint: "I used to work for twelve hours in my tiny shop mending stockings, and even though my eyes needed some rest in the evening, needlepoint was never a burden; on the contrary, it helped me get through all sorts of problems that had been going on." Problems, unfortunately, were not in short supply for Ana in the 1990s. While her son and his family were preparing to leave the country, Ana's husband was hit by a car while walking to pick her up from her workshop. Three months later, he died from injuries sustained in the accident. Shortly after his father's death, Ana's son left the country for good. In the space of three months, Ana went from living with her husband, son, daughter-in-law, and two little grandchildren to being completely alone. During the day, she busied herself with work and talking to some of her long-standing clients who had become friends over the years. Upon returning home, tapestries offered comfort in her solitude and sadness caused by the sudden departure from her life of everyone she loved. Again, just as with Mirjana, each stitch Ana made was not only a stitch in the actual fabric but an intervention into the weaving of memories—some she wanted to remember and others she created to replace the unwanted ones.

Ana's tapestries hung on the wall in the living room and the bedroom. The magnificent Wiehler's *Last Supper* tapestry adorned the central wall in the small living room. It had taken Ana years to complete this elaborate Gobelin tapestry. Below the tapestry, an open cupboard displayed china and crystal, in front of which stood a row of photographs. Half of the photos showed two children, whereas the others portrayed an attractive young woman. The children's pictures were unframed and just leaning against a crystal glass. The first photo showed a four- or five-year-old girl and a two- or three-year-old boy. As I picked up this photo for a closer look, I discovered more recent photos behind the older ones. Ana explained that this first photograph showed her grandchildren as they were before emigrating and that this was how she remembered them. She pointed to other pictures and commented that the children had grown and changed a lot. Next to this one was a photo of her son and his wife, taken in Australia.

However, I still had no clue about the young woman in some of the other photographs. Ana explained that this was her lodger, Maja, a young medical doctor who had been living with her for several years. Even though Maja was paying for her accommodation, their relationship was more than that between a landlady and a boarder. Ana talked about her with great pride, boasting of what an excellent student Maja was, how she even finished an MPhil in medicine, how she worked as a doctor in the neighborhood, and how all the neighbors praised her as an excellent and empathetic physician. Maja's photos stood right next to those of Ana's son and his family. Still, Maja's were the only recent photographs on display that corresponded to Ana's present life. It would be stretching things to say that a lodger had replaced her son. Nonetheless, in terms of the space she occupied in the apartment, as well as her importance in Ana's life—all her friends knew about the tenant and her talents, as well as about Maja's romantic relationship with "an unworthy layabout" that was bothering Ana—Maja's presence was much more prominent than that of just a tenant. The layout of photographs, the space they occupied, and how Ana arranged them according to her references to present and past seemed to give evidence to the greater attachment she had for her current lodger than for anyone in her past.

Similarly to Mirjana, Ana had minimal contact with her son and his family after their emigration. According to Ana, her daughter-in-law contributed to her somewhat strained relationship with her son and his family. Although her daughter-in-law's mother had gone several times to Australia, Ana had never visited her son and his family. Not that she could afford to travel—her difficult financial situation prevented her from doing so. But she was hurt because her son had never even invited her to come and visit them. She sold whatever she could from her family inheritance and sent all the money to her son and his family. During the ten years since they had emigrated, Ana's son and his family had visited her only once.

The layout of her grandchildren's photos, with more recent ones tucked behind the older ones that Ana had personal memories of, suggested her reluctance to accept the fact that she was not a part of her grandchildren's lives. Ana wanted to preserve the memory of her grandchildren from the time they lived with her, and she struggled to relate to the teenagers that she saw in the more recent photographs. While she did not articulate this bluntly like Mirjana, it was clear that Ana considered her teenage grandchildren strangers because she had no shared experience with them. They were the token grandchildren. She was indeed proud of their academic achievements, but a dose of resentment was evident in the concealed photos of her grandchildren as teenagers.

It was not a coincidence, then, that the only photos depicting recent events were those of her boarder, Maja. It was with Maja that Ana had established a relationship more akin to that between family, transcending the formality of a landlady-lodger relationship. Ana needed someone to talk to and care for, and in the absence of her family, a tenant was a welcome substitute. Unlike Mirjana, who created her new family in tapestries, growing them stitch after stitch with her hands, Ana found a different way of creating a familial, motherly relationship with this young woman, whom she had taken in as a lodger because her pension was not enough to cover the cost of living.

Home Is Where the Children Are

Milutin and Ljiljana were both in their early eighties at the time of my field-work in 2006.[22] They lived in a spacious three-bedroom apartment in central Belgrade. Milutin was a retired director of one of the Yugoslav utility companies, and Ljiljana was a retired engineer. Milutin's position allowed their family to enjoy a lavish lifestyle by Yugoslav standards. This, however, could not last forever. As their children became adults and started their own families in the 1980s, they encountered economic crisis and unemployment. Petar, their son, got married and worked as a taxi driver in the 1980s; his wife worked as a clerk. They faced a much harsher reality than Petar and his sister had experienced growing up as offspring of a privileged socialist company director. Petar and his wife decided to emigrate from Belgrade to the United States in 1990. At the time, Petar's children were eight and five years old. His younger sister, Sonja, had gone through several marriages, and at the time of my fieldwork in 2006 was divorcing her third husband. She had moved back to her parents' home with her five-year-old son.

Milutin and Ljiljana lived in a 1930s apartment that consisted of a salon, three bedrooms, a dining room, and an open-plan kitchen with high ceilings that enhanced the impression of spaciousness. When their daughter moved back in with them, Milutin and Ljiljana moved to their son's room because, as they said, they needed less space than their daughter. Sonja's five-year-old son, Ognjen, was in the room that had once belonged to his mother when she was a child. Several photographs of Ognjen hung in the salon; some of his photos were also in the dining room, along with two pictures of Nikola and Irena, two other grandchildren who lived in America. The apartment had been mainly adjusted to accommodate the needs of its youngest resident. There were few traces of Milutin and Ljiljana's other grandchildren in the apartment. Milutin explained that he was happy that his daughter did not want to live in the United States and that she had decided to stay in Belgrade; if she had not, he and his wife would have had to move to America as well because his wife would insist on being near her children.

Milutin described in great detail the material aspects of their son's life in Los Angeles. I learned about his son's house, his family's weekly grocery shopping, the different kinds of dairy products they bought in comparison to what his parents could afford in Serbia, his son's career progression, as well as about his grandchildren and their educational and career achievements. When he started describing how he had taught Petar to make sauerkraut in Los Angeles, Ljiljana blushed and interrupted him, saying that was not important. Unlike Milutin, who talked about material things related to their son's migration, Ljiljana seemed embarrassed by the way her husband spoke about their migrant son and his family. She spoke of her mixed feelings, how she was happy because her son's family had a better life in the United States, but at the same time she seemed profoundly sad:

> I went through a difficult period when they left. . . . Time is a great healer, and I was glad that they were happy and that they had each other there. The relationship with them stayed very much alive, and I hope it will remain like that in the future. Life goes on, and we have to adapt to new circumstances. I am glad that our children are still fond of us, but it is certain that there is sorrow because they are far away. You know—when it's tough, you would like them to be there to talk to them. Then I call them just to hear their voice. But that is so sad.

Ljiljana paused at that point. Her eyes welled with tears. Milutin did not speak either. The silence around us became almost physical as I witnessed aged parents crushed by grief and pain over their loss. Even though they still had each other—unlike Milena, Mirjana, and Ana, who were divorced or widowed and with no other children near them—Milutin and Ljiljana shared a lot in common with those mothers. The most significant difference in their case was the presence of their daughter and grandson. While Mirjana created her own family in the form of tapestries, and Ana developed a close, almost familial relationship with her lodger, Ljiljana and Milutin busied themselves with their young grandson and with helping their daughter find her footing after separating from her husband. But the burning emptiness remained for their absent son and grandchildren, with whom they had once been able to play and take for walks in a nearby park. Ljiljana's sadness over the loss of her son and grandchildren was as palpable as Milutin's detailed descriptions of the material evidence of their son's prosperity in his new world. In this respect, Ljiljana's experience of loss was no different from that of Milena, Mirjana, or Ana. Each mother longed to see her children and grandchildren, touch them, and hear their voices resonate in their homes. They yearned for the experience of being part of their children's and grandchildren's lives. They desired to be mothers and grandmothers.

The very few fathers in this research had a markedly different view of their children's migration. Like Milutin, they were incredibly proud of their children's successes and material achievements. However, it is difficult to draw any conclusions from these few examples because there were no single fathers in this research to compare to the experiences of a number of single mothers with whom I worked. All the fathers I met still had wives, and this made all the difference: they had not experienced the double loss of a partner and a child, as most of my female informants had.

Memories Undone

There is a certain complementariness between the richness of mothers' visual and verbal accounts of their children's lives, the liveliness and passion with which they narrate them, and the pain and emptiness caused by separation. It seems as if they are trying to furnish the physical absence of loved ones with countless photographs, as well as by performing certain rituals similar to practices related to remembering the deceased. This practice was directly connected to mothers' insistence on their son or daughter *leaving* and not *emigrating*. Whereas emigration suggests permanence, to say that someone has left implies the possibility of a return. This return for which mothers long is possible only in their memories, however. It is a return to a moment in the past that will never be repeated in the future. What mothers want to preserve, by feeding their insatiable memories through everyday interactions with objects reminiscent of their children, is also a memory of their own past. "Memories," writes Gaston Bachelard, "are motionless, and the more securely they are fixed in space, the sounder they are."[23]

While their sons or daughters are absent, and while there is some possibility, even an imaginary one, of their return, mothers preserve their rooms like museums that serve as memorials of their past, their motherhood, and the family that they raised. They keep objects that belonged to their children even when their sons and daughters do not want them. One mother, whose daughter emigrated to Canada with her family in the 1990s, admitted that she was unable to throw away her daughter's books and notebooks from elementary school, even after her daughter had told her to do so. The daughter's items reminded the mother of a time when she walked her daughter to school as a little girl, and she could not let go of them.

Photographs of migrant children and their families are there both for the mothers and for the public—relatives, friends, and neighbors—to create the (visual) presence of their absent children. Jean-Pierre Warnier argues that photographs, as well as all material objects due to their relative permanence, "help the psyche in its work of establishing duration, memory and sense of continuity."[24] Several examples of parents' homes in

Belgrade illustrated this point. Furthermore, these examples show that the relationship between parents and children was not only deeply rooted in the material culture of home but also came into existence through people's movement through space—what Warnier terms "motoricity."[25] Repeating choreographed movements through one's home reiterated one's role as a mother. The ritual of doing things around home that a mother would do affirmed one's identity as a mother, even, or perhaps especially, when there was no one else to witness it.

Daily embodied practice, according to Pierre Bourdieu, produces a worldview; this worldview, argues Warnier, could be embedded, material-ized, and worked on through processes of containment.[26] In other words, the practices that mothers performed in their homes were material and embodied manifestations of their subjectivity. DeVault's work has shown that families are created through the work that constitutes them—through caring, providing for, and taking into account the needs of each family member.[27] When children left home in the 1990s, some of them never to return, this was the beginning of an end to the family in which they had grown up. They were adults off to a new world, a new life, creating new families. For mothers left behind, this was the beginning of a new kind of family work. They constructed their motherhood through engagement with the material world of the home, through rituals, stitching, and embod-ied practices performed daily in the intimacy of home. Even when children were long gone and had limited contact with their mothers, the making and remaking of the material world of the home remained an active stage for discursive practices of motherhood. The making of motherhood brought comfort, anxiety, anger, and sadness, but above all, it created a still, tranquil moment when everything else was falling apart. Mothers' entire familiar world crumbled in the chaos of the 1990s and became unrecognizable. And with their children gone indefinitely overseas, the material world of home and the making of motherhood remained one of the few anchors in their lives.

Notes

1. One mother that I met through contact with her London-based daughter preferred to meet me in a café in central Belgrade, and the other mother lived in a town outside Belgrade and suggested meeting with me when she came to Belgrade on other business.

2. See Butler, *Gender Trouble*; and DeVault, *Feeding the Family*.

3. DeVault, *Feeding the Family*, 39.

4. Parents corrected me on several occasions to state that their children had not "emigrated" but had "departed" or "left." More than once I heard a mother say, for example, "When my daughter left on March 5, 1992 . . ." or "I will never forget how cloudy and miserable it was on October 27, 1993, when my son departed." The verb "departed" has a similar double meaning in Serbian as in English, denoting both "left" and "passed away." People often used this term to emphasize the effect their children's migration had on them—a feeling of permanent loss.

5. This notable exception was Sanja, a woman from Belgrade who came to London with her fiancé, Milan, in the 1990s. Milan escaped the military draft and came to London to continue with his university education. By the time of my fieldwork in 2005–06, Sanja had already lost both her parents. The photos of her parents and other family members were visibly displayed in Sanja and Milan's London home. Moreover, Sanja noted that the house bore a memory of her father because he had helped them a lot with a makeover. She pointed out specifically which projects her father had done, emphasizing his tireless work and the love he had invested in her home. Sanja, interview by author, London, November 25, 2005.

6. Milena, interview by author, Belgrade, May 23, 2006. As part of the socialist legacy in Serbia, most people used the living room as a bedroom or, by adding a sofa bed, used it as both a living room and bedroom. In this case, a four-bedroom apartment would mean three bedrooms and a living room.

7. The Amnesty Law was finally passed in 2006 because of the backlog of cases asking to drop charges against men who had evaded conscription in the 1990s. Thousands of young men who fled Serbia to resist going to the front in the 1990s were able to visit their home country only after April 2006. Milena's son had not yet been back at the time of my fieldwork in 2006. Milena suffered severe health problems in subsequent years and, unfortunately, I lost contact with her.

8. Milena's was the only case I encountered in Belgrade in which a parent was receiving regular financial help from children abroad. Milena explained that her pension could not cover the upkeep of the apartment, and because her children insisted that she does not sell the apartment, they all agreed that her son and daughter would send money for the monthly bills.

9. Edwards, "Photographs as Objects of Memory," 222.

10. Ibid.

11. Berger, *Understanding a Photograph*, 20.

12. Pamuk, *Istanbul*, 10.

13. Ibid., 12.

14. DeVault, *Feeding the Family*.

15. Mirjana, interview by author, Belgrade, May 24, 2006.

16. I found this unusual because in most of the homes I visited during fieldwork, there was seldom anything hanging in corridors. Hallways were considered to be a transient space where one did not stop or pay attention to the wall decorations.

17. Naji, "Gender and Materiality," 68.

18. Burguiere, "Le concept d'autocontrainte," cited in Naji, "Gender and Materiality," 69.

19. Naji, "Gender and Materiality," 70.

20. Ana, interview by author, Belgrade, May 17, 2006.

21. Ana was repairing women's nylons (hosiery), as these were expensive and difficult to source during the socialist period. The post-socialist period in Serbia pushed women into an even more precarious situation where they struggled to feed their families and where

buying new nylons still posed a significant challenge. Ana was still repairing nylons in the post-Milošević's era of the early 2000s, a stark reminder about the depth and longevity of economic crisis that started in 1992.

22. Milutin and Ljiljana, interview by author, Belgrade, May 19, 2006.

23. Bachelard, *The Poetics of Space*, 9, cited in Hallam and Hockey, 79.

24. Warnier, "A Praxeological Approach," 17.

25. Ibid., 6.

26. Bourdieu, *The Logic of Practice*; Warnier, "Inside and Outside," 188–91.

27. DeVault, *Feeding the Family*.

4

INALIENABLE POSSESSIONS

Serbian Remittances

WHEN I ARRIVED IN BELGRADE IN MAY 2006 for the second part of my fieldwork with families of the 1990s migrants, I encountered a few surprises. One unexpected revelation was the discrepancy between the ethnographic reality and that described by the media, which claimed that around USD 4–5 billion arrived annually in Serbia in the form of remittances. During my previous eight months of fieldwork in London, I had not uncovered anything to support that assertion. In fact, only one of my forty informants in London had been sending money to her family in Belgrade. Likewise, in my Belgrade fieldwork, remittances did not play a prominent role. Despite spending hours day after day in my informants' homes, I detected no sign of remittances: they were never mentioned, nor did I see evidence of additional income within their households. Most of the women I worked with lived in small apartments built in socialist-era concrete apartment blocks furnished with appliances that were thirty years old on average. What I did witness was the loneliness of elderly mothers who talked for hours on end about their loss, their migrant children, and the emptiness—physical and emotional—that remained in the wake of their children's departure.[1]

All the while, Serbian newspapers' bombastic headlines about the alleged billions of dollars pouring into the country from the diaspora fueled people's imaginations of fortunate parents whose children were sending them money from abroad.[2] And although I did not witness remittances reaching my informants, I wanted to address this issue with them because it featured so prominently in the public discourse. I discovered that remittances represented a taboo for Belgrade mothers. Elderly mothers in Belgrade considered it unacceptable to receive material support from children, and the very question of whether they received money from their migrant sons and daughters abroad embarrassed my informants.[3] They blushed, looked away, and explained that they had not given birth to their children expecting to be supported them. In the few cases where mothers received remittances, they insisted that the money was not used for everyday consumption. They made a clear distinction between the money that their son or daughter sent occasionally and the remittances that *gastarbajteri* doing temporary work in Germany in the 1970s and 1980s sent to their families. To Belgrade-based elderly mothers, receiving financial support or a gift with a value that was not purely symbolic was something that only peasants could accept.[4] The appropriate gift for a mother-child relationship, according to my informants, was a present with little or no material value, one that was symbolic and inalienable. Money thereby became a circulating form of inalienable gift that mothers saved so that their children would get it back as their inheritance. The only exception was when it was used for a purpose that transcended consumption, such as treating severe illness or paying funeral costs. A gift that came from a child—a sacred object of a mother's love and care—could not be used for mundane things.

One might ask where the money recorded in statistics on Serbian remittances was going if so many Belgrade parents denied receiving it. One explanation is that the majority of payments to Serbia were channeled to the same recipients as in the 1970s and 1980s—that is, to the families of *gastarbajteri*. The post-1990 generation of migrants who originated mostly from urban parts of Serbia remitted much less, either because they did not think they should do so or because their families did not expect them to. These qualitative findings have been corroborated by quantitative data from the 2011 census in Serbia, which shows that people over the age of sixty from the Belgrade area received the lowest volume of remittances in the country.[5]

The Contested Gift

Just as mothers instinctively knew what gifts were proper to accept from a migrant child, they were quite explicit about what gifts were appropriate to send. For example, mothers commonly sent their grandchildren sweets and snacks. Apart from food, mothers also sent money. It was entirely fitting for mothers to send money—money was a contested gift only when sent from children to mothers. This practice seemed to be an utter incongruity, as in many cases it was the mothers who were in real financial need; being able to send fifty dollars was an effort involving months of saving and deprivation. It was just as typical to come across such cases as it was to hear that they had not taken a vacation in fifteen years; they had a thirty-year-old car they could not afford to drive; the last household appliance they had bought was twenty years old; they had stopped eating meat and fish because they could not afford them; their diet consisted of bread, milk, potatoes, beans, and cabbage; or that they lived on credit because their pensions did not cover even the essential monthly bills. And yet at least once or twice a year, these mothers would send fifty, a hundred, or sometimes even two hundred dollars as a gift to their son, daughter, or grandchildren.

Such was the case of Ana, whom we met in chapter 3. Ana's material circumstances were quite dire. She received the minimum state pension, which was not enough to cover her monthly bills, and, despite her advanced age and cataracts that affected her eyesight badly, Ana still occasionally took on some work to supplement her pension. She also rented out the only bedroom in her apartment and slept on a couch in the living room. Undeterred by her struggle to meet basic needs, Ana still tried to send some money to her grandchildren in Australia. Whenever she heard that someone she knew was going to Australia, she sent a letter to her son and USD 50 for her grandchildren to buy chocolate from Grandma. Ana was not on good terms with her daughter-in-law, who had embarrassed her the last time people had brought a gift from Ana. She had wanted the people who carried the letter to go and see her son's house. Because she had never seen it herself, she wanted her "messengers" to see how her son lived and then tell her about it when they came back from Australia. But this did not happen, and the doors of her son's house had remained closed to Ana's friends. Despite her disappointment, Ana's love for her son was boundless:

> My son travels a lot because of the nature of his work, and I can't blame him. His wife is disrespectful, and I think I will stop sending anything. He knows that I am struggling to make ends meet with my pension, and now and then he asks me if I need help. But I would never ask him for help. I'd rather find my ways of surviving than receive money from him. I was trying to get pregnant for thirteen years . . . for thirteen years I was waiting to have a baby. My son came as a gift from God. There is no way I could ever accept anything from him because he is so special to me.

Ana's comment that she had not given birth to her son expecting him to be "useful" and to support her financially was not an exception in my fieldwork. The "sacred child" theme dominated mothers' discourses about their children's migration. During my fieldwork in Belgrade, I came across several cases in which mothers were receiving remittances from sons or daughters. Nonetheless, except for Milena from the previous chapter, they did not use the money for everyday consumption. The money coming from a sacred child could be used only for specific purposes and only after all other means had been exhausted.

When I contacted Ana after the end of my fieldwork in summer 2006, she told me that her son and his family had visited her for the first time since they had left for Australia. She was overjoyed. Even though she was struggling for survival and had severe diabetes, Ana spent several days cooking and preparing for their visit. Her son told her that they had two houses in Australia, one in which they lived and a second one that they rented out; they were about to buy an apartment to rent out as well. He was shocked to learn that his mother had sold all her family jewelry because she had no money to pay for diabetes injections. She never complained to him on the phone or revealed the gravity of her financial situation. And since he never came to visit her, he had no idea how poor his mother had become during the years he had been in Australia. Ana told him that she was about to sell her apartment because she needed money to pay for her medical treatment. On hearing this, Ana's son begged her not to sell the apartment because he wanted to have a place to stay when he came to Belgrade; he offered instead to send her money monthly for her diabetes medications. Ana agreed, as it was the only solution left. This, however, proved to be an empty promise: since returning to Australia, Ana's son had not sent a single payment toward his mother's medications, and Ana was forced to find a new lodger.

Like Ana, Milica was a widow in her seventies, and she lived alone in an apartment building in New Belgrade.[6] She was particular about the gifts or financial help that she received from her daughter in London. It was only during the period of hyperinflation and shortages in 1993 and 1994 that Milica received material support from her daughter, mostly in the form of food and hygiene and cleaning products:

> In those years there was no air traffic because of the sanctions, so my daughter had to fly from London to Budapest and then take a bus to Belgrade, bringing us food, cleaning products, and other basic things that we didn't have here, like soaps, shampoos, toothpaste, deodorants, washing powder. And again, when her father was diagnosed with cancer a year ago, she was paying for the treatment because we couldn't afford it . . . she also paid for his funeral. She adored her father. They had a special bond. She knew the exact moment when

he passed away. She came back home from work in London, sat down to have a coffee and a cigarette, looked at the icon on the wall and saw her father's image. She phoned me from London to say that she knew that Dad had just passed away.

Svetlana, another widow in her seventies, had two sons in the United States.[7] Her younger son came back to visit her in 1993, flying to Vienna and from there continuing by bus to Belgrade as there were no flights to Serbia because of the UN embargo. Svetlana recalled the glorious sight of her son entering her apartment "loaded like Father Christmas" with hygiene and cleaning products as well as the food they could not buy because of the hyperinflation. Even when the situation improved, Svetlana's son continued to send money—not only to her but to his uncle, her sister and brother-in-law, and their daughter: "He spends a lot on us. And I know that he doesn't earn a lot; he lives quite modestly. I don't use that money but put it in the bank. I have two savings accounts that the two of them [her sons] will inherit one day when I die. I don't want to spend their money unless something happens, like an illness or if I need to have an operation. I don't want to be a burden to them. I prefer selling one of my husband's paintings if I need the money."

Mothers were adamant that they did not expect anything in return from their sons and daughters. When I implied that Serbia was one of the top remittance-receiving countries in Europe, mothers became defensive. Awaiting money from migrant children, according to my informants, was typical of peasants who had a different attitude to children than parents in urban areas. Since the 1960s, *gastarbajteri* had been known to send money back to their families in rural parts of Yugoslavia. Their families built houses that remained either unfinished or empty, waiting for the guest workers to retire and return to live in them. These practices, however, were seen as typical of the working class, from which the majority of *gastarbajteri* had originated.

In other cases, Belgrade parents became apologetic—as in the case of Danica, whose daughter and son had migrated to the United States in the mid-1990s:[8]

I don't know how to explain this to you; we are so modest . . . [pause] we would never ask for anything from our children. We are not the kind of people who look or behave like they have children in America. We can't say they don't care about us; they do, and they want to buy us this and that, but look at me—I am a simple person, I don't need much. And we tell them not to bring anything to us. Maybe young people here care about branded clothes or perfumes, and they should have them. We don't want or need anything. The only thing that we accepted was money for medical treatment because my husband suddenly got very ill and he couldn't walk anymore. Our daughter wanted to make sure that we had the money if we had to take him to a hospital.

Danica reiterated that it was not that their children were irresponsible or neglected them; she and her husband did not want to be a burden to their children. Danica and her husband lived on their pensions, which, as she explained, were not good but were at least better than the minimum state pension. They were old, she said; they did not smoke or drink, and they did not buy anything new. They were cautious about how they spent their modest pensions. Their migrant children reminded them not to deprive themselves but to buy whatever they wished or needed. And because they would not use their children's money, and their pensions were too small for purchasing any household goods, their children would buy new things for the house when they came to visit. Danica recounted that when her daughter-in-law wanted to clean their apartment, she realized their thirty-year-old vacuum cleaner was falling apart and decided to buy them a new one. Likewise, when Danica's daughter came to visit them, she noticed their washing machine was broken and bought them a new one. These essential things, Danica explained, which made their life more comfortable but which they could not afford, were the kind of material help they received from their migrant children.

Nonmigrant Children

Mothers of adult migrants who had another child in Belgrade did not treat the latter any differently. They considered it their duty as mothers to make sacrifices for their children, near or far, regardless of how old and impoverished they had become. As the majority of young people in Serbia in the early 2000s could not afford to rent or buy an apartment, it was common in my fieldwork to come across households where the remaining child and her family all lived in the same parental home. Not only were parents providing their children and grandchildren with accommodation, but they also cooked, cleaned, and often looked after their grandchildren.

Desa had a daughter in the United States and a son who had stayed in Belgrade.[9] Since the son could not afford to move away and his mother could not help him financially, they split Desa's two-bedroom apartment in half and added a separate entrance door. Neighbors in Desa's block of apartments were surprised when they saw another door in the hallway. They gossiped that Desa's son was manipulating his mother and that what he had done was outrageous. However, Desa maintained that it was her wish to help her children as much as she could; she could not stand to see her son struggle in a tiny rented apartment while she was on her own in a two-bedroom apartment. Desa was a retired widow, and since she had no savings, the only thing she could leave to her son and daughter was her apartment. "One day when I die, my daughter will inherit my half of the apartment so that she has a place to stay when she visits from America," she remarked.

It was not uncommon for Belgrade parents to sell their apartments to help their children solve housing problems or facilitate their migration. Dragan and Jelica were both retired and lived in a small apartment in New Belgrade.[10] For years, Dragan had worked as a director in one of the Yugoslav state-owned companies, which had allocated to him a large apartment befitting his high-ranking position. After the fall of Yugoslavia, Dragan and Jelica bought the apartment from the company. When their daughter decided to immigrate to Canada in the 1990s, Dragan and Jelica sold their apartment and bought two smaller ones—one for them and the other for their son. They gave the remaining money to their daughter so that she had something to live on until she found a job and settled down in Toronto. In the meantime, both their daughter in Toronto and their son in Belgrade got married and had children. Dragan and Jelica spent at least three months every year in Toronto helping their daughter with childcare. The rest of the time they were in Belgrade, looking after their son's children.

Milutin and Ljiljana, whom we met in chapter 3, had a son, Petar, in Los Angeles and a daughter, Sonja, who lived in Belgrade. While Sonja was married, Ljiljana went to her daughter's home every day to look after her grandson, Ognjen. After the divorce, as a single mother, Sonja found it easier to move back in with her parents because they could help her with childcare. Even though Milutin and Ljiljana were about eighty at the time of my research, they still went to the market for groceries, cooked, cleaned, and walked their grandson to and from the nursery. According to Milutin, he had spent his savings on his son's immigration to America. They had no funds left to help their daughter financially, so they tried to compensate by helping her out in other ways. The only thing they had left to give was themselves, and that they gave selflessly.

Similarly to Milutin and Ljiljana, Olivera had one daughter in London and another in Belgrade.[11] The one in Belgrade was divorced and, like Sonja, she had moved in with her mother after the divorce. The daughter had married very young, explained Olivera, and did not have time to study because of the baby. While married, her daughter had lived in Montenegro because her husband was from there. After the divorce, her daughter moved back to Serbia, and since she could not afford to support herself and her daughter, they moved in with Olivera and her mother, whom Olivera looked after as well since she was too old to live by herself. Olivera was confident that her daughter could finish her studies because she was there to help with childcare and housework. Having four women of four different generations in one household was not easy, noted Olivera, but she had to help her mother, her daughter, and her granddaughter: "I did the same for my other daughter in London when she had a baby. I am their mother, and it is my duty to help my children," she explained. This sense of duty for one's children, regardless of their age, financial circumstances, or geographical distance, defined a mother's role for most of my Belgrade informants.

In short, the sacrifices that mothers—and, in a few cases, fathers—made for their absent children were no different from those they performed for their nonmigrant children. The fact that the mothers belonged to the old Yugoslav middle class but had experienced severe downward mobility in the 1990s and the fact that their children abroad, even if they had low-paying jobs, were likely to have a much better living standard than their mothers today were the aspects that made mothers' sacrifice toward migrant children seem irrational to anyone else but themselves. To a mother, it only seemed right to do the same thing for an absent child as for one who was present. It was their absence that made a sacrifice for a son or daughter abroad stand out. A sacrifice for a nonmigrant adult child and his or her family seemed quite logical because they were often struggling with work, could not afford to rent or buy an apartment, and needed help with childcare. Elderly mothers, therefore, considered it their duty to take care of nonmigrant children, even if they were in their thirties or forties. Thus, everything that mothers could not do on a daily basis for their absent children and their families accumulated into what represented the ultimate sacrifice for them—sending money to their children and grandchildren abroad instead of accepting a remittance from them.

Narratives of Class Trajectories

Even though the women in the preceding examples were not in the same financial situation—some were barely surviving, while others were much better off—what they had in common was an understanding that, if received, remittances should not be consumed for mundane purposes because they came from their children, whom they considered sacred objects of love and care. This attitude toward children was typical of the generation of women born around the time of World War II and who belonged, in their view, to the middle class.

Sociologist Anđelka Milić identifies motherhood as the most essential aspect of identity among women in socialist Yugoslavia. Her research demonstrates that women in the former Yugoslavia worked and lived for their children.[12] Marina Blagojević terms this behavior "self-sacrificing micromatriarchy."[13] Women, according to Blagojević, acquire a sense of power within the home sphere through sacrifice for their home, family, and children.[14] However, Milić argues that this seemingly "self-sacrificing" behavior was a consequence of the socialist project of women's emancipation—while women were stimulated to pursue education and employment, they were not free from traditional patriarchal norms of having a primary responsibility for their families and children. Employment and (relative) financial independence, according to Milić, enabled women to feel respected for their work in the domestic sphere, if not so much by their husbands, then by their social circle and, above all, their children.[15] The fall of Yugoslavia and massive emigration of adult children that coincided with a change of social norms and values created this incredibly difficult situation for elderly mothers. With the abrupt changes in values and departure of their children, their world collapsed: no one was left in the inner social circle or family to appreciate women's sacrifice. Elderly mothers felt, perhaps more than anyone else, a literal crumbling of socialist values—they lost everything in this process, including their identity.

The case of the Serbian middle class resonates with Jennifer Patico's study of consumption in the post-Soviet middle class, in which those who defined themselves as such did so based on being born and socialized within middle-class families and a middle-class milieu during the Soviet period. This group appropriated "middle-class" identity in post-Soviet times even though its members "found it increasingly difficult to conceive of themselves that way given their positions in a new market in commodities and labor."[16] The socialist middle class in post-socialist Serbia, like its Russian counterpart, had become impoverished, but people still defined themselves as middle class based on their culturedness.[17] Even though the former occupations of my informants in Belgrade varied substantially in terms of income (retired teacher, seamstress, company director, translator, housewife), they all had in common the fact that they lived and raised their children in Belgrade, socializing them into the socialist middle-class identity and providing the education and skills that subsequently facilitated their children's emigration. The comparison with the Russian self-professed middle class, the diversity of backgrounds—with many urban dwellers in Serbia coming from the countryside—as well as very different occupations ranging from blue- to white-collar work to unemployment, points to the fact that the class discourse in Belgraders' context was highly subjective.[18] In other words, appropriating a middle-class identity was the result of an active process of self-positioning and constructing one's culturedness in opposition to the Other, embodied as the peasant.

Socialism had tried hard to dismantle peasantry—in a country where the majority of the population was of peasant origin—as it did not fit within the parameters of the classless society it claimed to be. The peasant was systematically constructed as the enemy within during both the socialist and post-socialist periods. During socialism, a peasant was portrayed sympathetically as a naïve, warmhearted, uncultured relative from the countryside. As the war blazed through the former Yugoslavia, the term *peasant* lost these positive connotations. In addition to "uncultured," the meaning of the term *peasant* in the 1990s amalgamated the anxieties of nationalism and the eroding socialist system of values—it stretched far beyond a symbol of someone who hailed from the countryside. It became an archetype of post-socialist aesthetics: turbo-folk music, fake Diesel jeans (an Italian brand), Nike trainers, and a thick gold chain with a cross. This new peasant lived for the moment and did not care what he did but how much he earned, even if this involved illegal activities in the flourishing black market. He was someone with no morals or regard for social values cultivated from the time of socialism. The peasant became an embodiment of the changes that swept away the familiar system of values and social norms. The middle class created this new peasant as a way of navigating the murky and tumultuous sea of post-socialist metamorphoses; the peasant was a counterbalance to a crumbling system of socialist middle-class values. As long as one could identify a peasant by his ways, one could hold on to middle-class values and ignore the reality that undermined one's middle-class identity.

Downwardly Mobile Parents

Even though the case of Serbian middle-class parents may seem extreme compared to the majority of other examples in the literature on remittances, this is a typical case of downward social mobility. One of the classic studies of downward mobility during the Great Depression in 1930s America shows that families tried to hide material deterioration from others by cutting back on less visible things and striving to maintain a public face seemingly untouched by poverty.[19] Another study has analyzed downwardly mobile American middle-class managers in the 1980s.[20] Because they did not expect to be out of work long, jobless parents refused to sell their houses and paid a high price for trying to preserve the false public image of their middle-class standard of living. As Katherine Newman poignantly argues, the downwardly mobile hold on tightly to their former professions, as these signify their position in society. The wallpaper would have peeled off long before they accepted the fact that they no longer belonged to the middle class: "Some cling to the old persona for years. When asked, they claim their previous occupations as engineers, vice presidents of marketing, or sales managers. . . . For the kids' sake, for the wife's sake, or simply for the sake of one's own sanity, it is hard to ditch yesterday's honored identity in order to make room for today's poor substitute."[21]

Food was one of the first things downwardly mobile families in 1980s America cut back on. No one outside an individual household would know whether its occupants were still eating steak or, instead, much cheaper junk food. This is reminiscent of many mothers in my Belgrade fieldwork, who became vegetarian because they could no longer afford meat and fish. As we see in chapter 2, pauper recipes, usually containing only a few of the most essential ingredients, proliferated in the 1990s as substitutes for more elaborate dishes. In most cases, mothers kept their migrant children unaware of the severity of their material circumstances, conforming to normative expectations.

The Social Meaning of Remittances

Serbian mothers' narratives about their migrant sons and daughters—seeing them as sacred objects from which they should only accept gifts of symbolic value—are evocative of Viviana Zelizer's study of the making of the "priceless child" in early-twentieth-century America.[22] Zelizer argues that a shift in constructing the "sacred child" emerged as a consequence of the massive industrialization in America at the turn of the last century. Gradually, the role of a child was transformed from a unit of labor, even priced as such (older children had higher value than younger ones), to an object of continuous parental sacrifice and unconditional love, a priceless child.[23] Along similar lines, Igor Kopytoff argues that material affluence in most modern industrial societies has allowed Westerners to "purge relations with kinsmen of much economic content and make them almost entirely 'social.'"[24] According to Kopytoff, parents in Western societies are in a position not to expect any material benefits from their children; this, however, is not the case in poor peasant societies, where arduous material conditions influence rather different relationships between parents and children.[25]

Industrialization in Serbia did not get fully underway until the mid-twentieth century, when Josip Broz Tito put Yugoslavia on the fast track to modernization.[26] Before World War II, 90 percent of the Serbian population were peasants, with families organized into collective households called *zadruga*.[27] The child in a *zadruga* was considered primarily as a unit of labor. There are documented cases in Serbia of families bribing teachers to overlook the fact that their children did not attend school because they were needed to work and maintain the household.[28] Once social reforms and rapid industrialization began in post–World War II Yugoslavia, the role of the child also began to change. The "priceless child" emerged to become a token of modernity.

It is interesting to see how this transformation was reflected in the case of migrants from Serbia. Before the fall of Yugoslavia and the massive exodus prompted by the conflict and by post-socialism, migration from Yugoslavia consisted mostly of *gastarbajteri* and, to a smaller degree, political and economic migrants. In the years before the collapse of Yugoslavia, economic migration of the young and educated had already started.[29] This trend was exacerbated in the 1990s because of the war and further deterioration of the economy. This brain drain diaspora differed from the previous generations of both *gastarbajteri* and the political émigrés who fled communism.[30]

The majority of Serbian *gastarbajteri* came from the countryside. Their remittance practices affirmed the class distinction between the "useful" children of peasants and the working class and the "priceless" children of the urban middle class.[31] For my informants, receiving remittances or other forms of financial support from a migrant child pointed to one's loss of middle-class status. It was a sign of post-socialist reordering and the end of the socialist class system.

During the last decade of the twentieth century, the socialist middle class of the Yugoslav period withered away. To be clear, it did not entirely disappear, but it stopped socially reproducing itself, giving way instead to a new post-socialist middle class. The socialist middle class had become so impoverished that it had become an empty signifier, clinging to class values that have become hollow in the new post-socialist class system in Serbia. Mothers of the old socialist middle class repudiated financial support from their migrant children even though they needed it, resisting the inexorable post-socialist social reordering. While the *gastarbajteri*, the old working class from Yugoslav times, found remittances unproblematic and continued to send them—indeed, they were the main contributors to the staggeringly large pool of remittances to Serbia as recorded by the World Bank in the mid-2000s—the old middle class felt this was just not an acceptable way for money to flow within family relationships, even though this rejection was to their detriment.

For these people, as for millions of other Eastern Europeans, the changes brought about by postcommunism meant, as Katherine Verdery describes, "a reordering of people's entire meaningful worlds; . . . a rupture in their worlds of meaning, their sense of cosmic order."[32] The new post-socialist classes in the 1990s, categorized as "poor" and "extremely rich," instigated new values and societal norms. Yet, the socialist middle class still clung to their old habits and beliefs, some of which manifested in their relationships with their children. The social norms relevant to these generations implied that mothers were there to protect children and look after them long into adulthood; they did not expect their children to sustain them or materially support them. This was considered something that peasants did, such as those who had *gastarbajter* sons in Germany, Austria, or Switzerland. The socialist urban middle class was there to support its migrant children in every possible way and not the other way around.

The piece of ethnography presented here gives strong support to Gil Eyal, Iván Szelényi, and Eleanor Townsley's argument about postcommunist transition following an involutionary path-dependent route.[33] The term "involutionary," first used by Clifford Geertz, describes the societal changes that do not follow an evolutionary path that implies progress but instead rely on old and familiar social patterns to adapt to new circumstances.[34] More recently, Eyal, Szelényi, and Townsley use this term to explain the transition of capital and power from communist to postcommunist conditions in Central Europe. This concept is valuable not only when studying how systems of power adapt but also when examining how individuals living in those systems adapt to new social circumstances. As we have seen in the examples described in this chapter, even though the material conditions of the old middle class indicated that they were not middle class anymore, people strove to maintain that position in society in any way possible. They might have been impoverished, but most of them still possessed substantial cultural capital.[35] Most of them also made a conscious decision, as a token of love for their sacred child, not to accept money from their migrant children despite the ostensible poverty in which they lived.

Notes

Sections of this chapter have previously appeared in "The Lost Matriarch: The Consequences of Remittances on Mother-Child Relationships in Urban Serbia," *Genero—Časopis za feministčku teoriju i studije kulture* 14 (2010): 25–48.

1. For comparison with Albanian emigration and its impact on elderly parents left behind, see King and Vullnetari, "Orphan Pensioners."

2. Mikavica, "Dosta šalju" [They send a lot]; Krivokapić, "Dijaspora pomaže" [Diaspora helps].

3. It should be noted that none of my research participants (in either London or Belgrade) used the word "remittances" (*doznake* in Serbian). Instead, they referred to remittances as "money" (*novac* or *pare* in Serbian). While there is no semantic difference in the meanings between the words "money" (e.g., a current medium of exchange in the form of coins and banknotes; financial gain; wage; assets) and "remittance," the word "remittance" in Serbia is used only officially, in banks and other institutions dealing with financial transactions. When one poses a question about remittances to mothers left behind, then, it is to ask if one receives money from children, and this bears a strong negative connotation.

4. See the introduction for a discussion about the social construction of "peasants" (*seljaci*).

5. Stanković, *Popis stanovništva* [Census of population]; according to the census data, most remittance recipients over sixty lived in South and Eastern Serbia (Ibid., 98).

6. Milica, interview by author, Belgrade, May 28. 2006.

7. Svetlana, interview by author, Belgrade, June 2, 2006.

8. Danica, interview by author, Belgrade, June 6, 2006.

9. Desa, interview by author, Belgrade, June 5, 2006.

10. Dragan and Jelica, interview by author, Belgrade, May 22, 2006.

11. Olivera, interview by author, Belgrade, June 2, 2006.

12. Milić, "Žene u bivšoj Jugoslaviji" [Women in former Yugoslavia], 195.

13. Blagojević, "Mladi i roditeljstvo" [Youth and parenthood], cited in Milić, "Žene u bivšoj Jugoslaviji" [Women in former Yugoslavia], 195.

14. Ibid.

15. Ibid.

16. Patico, *Consumption and Social Change*, 25.

17. Ibid., 26.

18. For an excellent discussion on class subjectivity, see Jansen, "Who's Afraid?"

19. See Komarovsky, *The Unemployed Man*.

20. See Newman, *Falling from Grace*.

21. Ibid., 10–11.

22. Zelizer, *Pricing the Priceless Child*.

23. Ibid.

24. Kopytoff, "Commoditizing Kinship," 273.

25. Ibid.

26. Perović, *Izmeđju anarhije i autokratije* [Between anarchy and autocracy].

27. Isić, "Dete i žena na selu u Srbiji" [Child and woman in Serbian village].

28. Ibid.

29. In the late 1980s, according to sociologist Ana Dević, young people under twenty-seven years of age comprised more than 70 percent of the total unemployed population in Yugoslavia ("What Nationalism Has Buried," 27).

30. Val Colic-Peisker, in *Migration, Class and Transnational Identities*, has brilliantly documented differences and misunderstandings between Croatian immigrants in Australia during the 1980s and 1990s and those who had settled in earlier decades. The "ethnics" struggled to understand the "cosmopolitans," who arrived in Australia with substantial cultural capital, armed with university degrees and proficiency in the English language, and slotted into the Australian middle class relatively seamlessly.

31. Zelizer, *Pricing the Priceless Child*.

32. Verdery, *Political Lives*, 35.

33. Eyal, Szelényi, and Townsley, *Making Capitalism*, 38–39.

34. Geertz, *Agricultural Involution*, cited in Eyal et al., *Making Capitalism*, 39.

35. Cultural capital, according to Pierre Bourdieu, encompasses education and skills acquired through work ("The Forms of Capital").

5

KEEPING IN TOUCH

"Can You Really Run Away from Sorrow?"

THE BEAUTY OF ETHNOGRAPHIC FIELDWORK, I DISCOVERED DURING my research in Belgrade in 2006, lies in the unexpected. Ethnographers often set out to investigate one phenomenon only to learn that they were mistaken about what they initially believed was relevant to the people they studied. My research was full of such discoveries. Instead of studying communication between migrants and their families left behind, the reality of fieldwork placed the focus of my research on the mothers left behind. Their experience of loss was incomparable to that of migrants. Staying put, I learned, was a much more difficult journey than emigrating. Elderly mothers were desperate to see their children and grandchildren, to be a part of their lives. But travel restrictions and strict visa regimes and their associated costs often resulted in mothers' isolation and a profound sense of loss—of both their loved ones and their own identity as mothers.

Mothers, however, were not resigned to their fate. They expressed tremendous resilience and creativity in their everyday routines and practices, trying to remind their children and themselves of who they were—mothers and women. Food mattered, as we have seen, not as a source of nourishment but as an embodied memory of a relationship between a mother and her adult children. Likewise, money sent to or saved for children and grandchildren abroad represented the ultimate sacrifice because the elderly mothers needed it much more than their adult migrant children. This complicated the simplistic assumption about the benefits of remittances for families left behind.

In accord with this realization—that nothing is what it seems to be at first glance—my assumption about communication technology being a tool for mothers and their migrant children to keep in touch also proved to be false. The prolonged crisis of the 1990s hindered technological advancement in Serbia. While some of my informants had a computer at home, in 2006 most of them still used a dial-up connection, as broadband was emerging in the market. The unreliable and slow connection did not allow for forms of simultaneous communication like Skype, so even the very few informants who had a computer and knew how to use it mainly wrote emails to their adult children abroad. Older informants, however, were unlikely to use technology because not only were computers too expensive, but they required a monthly internet subscription. To complicate matters even further, the software was in English, making learning it an obstacle for many older users. Although from the mid-2000s on, technology changed rapidly, becoming more affordable and user-friendly, at the time of my fieldwork in 2006, digital technology was still out of reach for most of my older informants.

Instead of digital communication, many of my informants relied on phone calls and letters. In the absence of international phone cards, elderly mothers usually waited for their migrant children to call them. To reach out to their migrant children, they would write letters. Letters, I discovered, were not just pieces of paper containing information about what went on in one's life at a particular point in time. The simplicity and open-endedness of a blank piece of paper gave mothers freedom to express themselves more intimately and creatively than through direct communication via phone. Mothers' handwriting was a reminder of themselves, often underlining their concentrated effort to instill a memory of the cursive Cyrillic alphabet in their migrant children. Recent family events and also newspaper clippings about things that mothers considered relevant for their migrant children featured in the letters. Letters, in other words, were carefully curated vessels for imparting knowledge and information, for instilling memories and bridging physical distance through the intimacy of expression and through the medium itself. This intimacy was conveyed through the choice of paper, the handwriting that reflected the physical changes one experienced in aging, and even through the envelope—often reused or saved from older, more affluent times.

Tracing paper was preferred because its thinness enabled mothers to fold it in half and squeeze multiple pages of dense handwriting into one letter; standard 80-gram paper was too thick and expensive for such missives. The handwriting functioned on two levels: it was a window into one's thoughts, but it also portrayed a very intimate image of one's physical body, giving away clues about ailments that plagued the writer. Cataracts, for example, manifested in letters written larger than usual, whereas tremors—the involuntary shaking of hands—appeared in slightly jagged lettering. Handwriting was a way of revealing the inevitable bodily changes that accompany old age without saying anything. This was the kind of intimacy that one would experience when living together—an implicit knowledge of gradual bodily transformations and failings. In this respect, letters were a much more powerful medium for creating intimacy than emails devoid of material properties. Like food and money, the materiality of a letter represented a physical extension of oneself. In a situation without years of physical contact, the ability to send an embodied extension of oneself in letters, food, or gifts was crucial for mothers left behind. It was their way of bridging the physical distance and connecting with their children's lives.

This was the case with Gordana, a retired pharmacist who was in her early eighties in 2006.[1] Gordana was widowed and lived by herself in a small studio apartment in New Belgrade, where she had moved in 1991 following the death of her husband. She had previously lived in Macedonia for thirty years, and when she relocated to Serbia, neither of her sons lived nearby. Her older son, Igor, had moved to the United States in the 1980s to get his PhD and pursue an academic career. Vanja, the younger son, had been living in Bosnia-Herzegovina with his wife in the early 1990s. When the war in Yugoslavia started, Vanja moved with his wife to the United States initially, then to Canada and back again to the United States. At the time of my fieldwork in 2006, both sons were living in the United States.

Gordana lived in the same block of apartments where I stayed during my fieldwork. Her straight back, proud bearing, swift gait, and piercing gaze left an impression of formidable strength and intelligence. In many ways, Gordana was exceptional among my informants. She was not too friendly with her neighbors, according to the gossip, even though she had lived in the building for fifteen years by the time of my fieldwork. She was polite and curt in the greetings she exchanged in passing with neighbors in the building, but no more than that. There were no coffees with neighbors and none of the customary prying into other's lives or gossiping about what went on in the building. She had one neighbor from her floor with whom she sometimes went for a walk, but otherwise she mostly kept to herself. Gordana stood aside from—if not to say above—the social life of her building.

Her neighbors had warned me not to expect much from an interview with Gordana, as she came across as a fiercely private person. There was a tinge of disbelief and envy in neighbors' gossip at Gordana's decision to open her door to an outsider and ethnographer, as most of them had never set foot in her home. In this respect, Gordana did not stand out from other mothers I worked with in Belgrade. Regardless of how social or private they were, one thing all mothers had in common was that they wanted to talk to me—not because of who I was but because they had a strong desire to share their stories without being judged.

Gordana did not treat me any differently than she treated her neighbors; she was polite but kept a distance. The usual offerings of coffee and cake were not forthcoming when I went to her home. Instead, she pointed immediately at a pile of papers lying across the table. These papers were the latest letter she was writing to Vanja. She wrote a few pages every day. The letter was already about fourteen pages long, Gordana explained, and she considered it would be ready in about ten days. She was using thin tracing paper folded in half, thus creating four pages out of one sheet of paper. The letters contained a summary of not only everything that happened to her but events in the political sphere, in the building where she lived, even bits of history or excerpts from books she was currently reading that she wished to share with her son. Gordana showed me a book of poems by well-known Yugoslav writer Branko Ćopić, explaining that she did not like his poems in general but that this one was an exception. "Listen to this," Gordana said, as she read three stanzas from "Odgovor zemljaku" [A Reply to a Compatriot] to me:

> And a dear old friend approached me,
> a reprimand-bitter like stone fell on me:
> "Eh, it seems, you have already forgotten us
> and you—have run away from Bosnia!"
>
> Oh, my good old Šefkete,
> if you say that, what will the others say?
> Is it that your heart-eye fools you, as well?
> And can you really run away from sorrow?
> . . .
> Bosnia even today leads my hand,
> and that thing about running away—please do not mention it ever again.
> Even when you leave, the old paths will haunt you.
> And can you really run away from sorrow?[2]

Gordana explained that this poem summarized the feeling of in-betweenness that one experiences after leaving one's homeland. "Perhaps it describes best how we who stayed behind feel about those who had left," added Gordana. Or perhaps, I wondered later on, this poem resonated with her own experience of migration from Bosnia? Gordana continued: "I also read somewhere that a migrant is happiest in the plane when he travels from one homeland to another. I liked that quote at the time, even though I didn't have the slightest idea that one day it would refer to my children. It's beautiful, isn't it?"

Gordana painstakingly collected sentences, poems, and pieces of writing that related to migration and exile and put them in her letters because she thought they would resonate with her sons' experience. She swiftly moved on to the next excerpt that was ready to be copied in the letter: "And listen to this, this is what [Jorge Luis] Borges wrote somewhere: 'having found his intimate homeland in migrating overseas, he didn't leave the impression that he had fulfilled everything he was dreaming about or that he had let go of everything which bothered him in the homeland.'³ Maybe you haven't come across this thought. I liked it. It refers to my children. You can't say that they are completely satisfied there or that they are longing for their homeland; it is more a discontent to mend something that is no longer whole."

Gordana's remarks about migration's impact on one's sense of ruptured identity sounded like they had come out of a textbook about migration. Already at this point in our conversation, it was evident that Gordana knew and felt more profoundly about this topic than most mothers I had met. The discussion about letter writing was a prelude to this mother's poignant account of her own experience of displacement, a vicarious atonement for explaining to her sons what she perhaps struggled to understand herself. In a way, Gordana was reliving different parts of her own migration experience through her sons, in particular that of Vanja, with whom she had a closer, more intimate relationship.

Gordana was born in the 1920s in Banja Luka to a middle-class Bosnian Serb family. She was fourteen when World War II broke out. Her family, Gordana explained, always treated everyone respectfully—Serbs, Croats, and Muslims alike. Sadly, she said, politics got between people. Gordana's uncle (her mother's brother) was among the officers close to Queen Marija and took part in the demonstrations on March 27, 1941, to protest the Nazi occupation of Bosnia.⁴ In April, a few days into the Nazi occupation of

Yugoslavia, the Kingdom of Yugoslavia collapsed, and Bosnia-Herzegovina became part of the newly formed Independent State of Croatia (Nezavisna Država Hrvatska [NDH]) supported by Nazi Germany and Fascist Italy.[5] As a punishment for her uncle's participation in the March 27 demonstrations in Banja Luka, Gordana and her family were captured by the pro-Nazi Croatian authorities and taken to a concentration camp:

> My father was a teacher, so everyone knew him; even though he wasn't out on the streets on March 27, people knew that his brother-in-law was there, and we were all taken away. Immediately as the war broke out, the NDH started to collect the Serbs in Banja Luka and take them to concentration camps. We were among the first five hundred people who were captured for the concentration camp. . . . They killed fourteen men from our group immediately there in Banja Luka. The rest of us were taken to a concentration camp in Slavonska Požega, across the river Sava. We left without anything, can you imagine? [pause] Nothing. [pause] We were put in twenty-eight barracks separated with barbed wire, [pause] what do I tell you? [pause] That whole night we were being inspected, [pause] my schoolteacher, who was also my best friend's father, was searching us. He took everything from us, money and gold, everything. [pause] We spent the whole night standing in front of the barracks, without anything to eat or drink, waiting to be stripped naked. [pause] I was shaking with cold and with fear. [pause] Finally, they let us into the barracks. We were sleeping on the ground, on a thin layer of straw underneath us. And the water, [pause] oh, [pause] the water was dripping from a pipe underneath the toilet. We had to collect that water for drinking, [pause] and there were more killings in this group. After a month spent in the concentration camp, we were transported to Serbia. [pause] We didn't know where to go or what to do.

Gordana continued her poignant account with their arrival in Belgrade. While recounting this harrowing experience, Gordana remained fully composed as always. She recalled her terrible hunger and the first meal they received in a refugee camp in Serbia—*paprikaš* (stew). It was the best meal of her life, Gordana said with a faint smile, despite the thick layer of grease that had jelled on top. The joy of being released from the concentration camp was soon overshadowed by the harsh reality of living as refugees in the middle of the war. Times were extremely hard in Serbia because it was under German occupation, and the war and poverty did not leave much hope for Serbian refugees from Bosnia. Her family drifted from town to town in search of employment or settlement before her father found a job as a teacher in Kragujevac. Gordana described the mixed feelings of relief, excitement, and disappointment when they finally found a new home:

> There was a row of houses for rent in one of the streets, and at the end of that row, we found a house. It was a new building. But we had absolutely

nothing—no beds, chairs, nothing. Another shock was that there was no bathroom in the house. It was outside, in the courtyard. In Banja Luka, we lived in a three-bedroom apartment with a bathroom, making it so hard to adapt to the new reality. I can't remember if we had a tap in the kitchen. Some Russian immigrants gave us two folding beds; one lady gave us a table and some chairs. It was 1941, German occupation, others were suffering as well and there was no aid for refugees. Nothing. It was war everywhere . . . only one thing prevailed. Our clothes, thanks to my mother. She took care that we looked perfectly dressed [pause]; it was like a camouflage [pause]; no one in school could believe that we were refugees when they would see us in clean, starched shirts or dresses. [pause] You know that [Isaac Bashevis] Singer novel where he says, '[We] never complained, never begged'?—It was like that.[6]

The war ended four years later, and Gordana graduated from high school. The family returned to their hometown, Banja Luka, in Bosnia, and once again they had nothing. Gordana was profoundly fond of Banja Luka. Although her parents had relatives in Sarajevo and Prijedor, they wanted to return to Banja Luka. "It was a beautiful place and those who lived there really loved it," she said. However, Gordana did not stay long in Banja Luka; she soon moved to Serbia again to study pharmacology at the University of Belgrade. After graduation, Gordana got married and moved to Macedonia with her husband, who was from there. Although she was not a refugee and this was an internal migration within socialist Yugoslavia, Gordana's experience of migration to Macedonia spoke of displacement:

I can't say that was foreignness, but I knew I was a foreigner, even though that was all Yugoslavia. I am Serb, and they are Macedonians. You always have to stand out at work; you have to work harder than them if you want them to accept you. And that is not exploitation. I understood it this way: if I stand out at work, then they can't have objections. And it's also good for them. So when you come to a foreign place, work hard if you want them to accept you. And another thing: do not comment! My husband was a big Yugoslav; he criticized everyone, including the Macedonians. I don't think that is right. You have to be careful and watch what you say. You are there, and that country did, um, not a favor, but something good for you by accepting you when you had a hard time. If there is something you dislike about the place, don't say it aloud—let them criticize themselves, and you keep silent. This is what I say to my children [pause]—be yourself but respect the place that has given you hospitality.

From here, Gordana made a full circle back to her sons' migrant experience in America. In her narrative, Gordana seamlessly drifted between the migrant experiences of her sons and herself. While she did not write to her sons about her grueling childhood experience, the careful selection of texts, poems, citations, and advice that Gordana included in her letters created intimacy and understanding that went beyond that of motherly concern. Gordana's traumatic memories from the concentration camp in World War II, her betrayed hopes of a better life as a refugee in Serbia and as a returnee in Bosnia, followed by life as a foreigner in Macedonia were all woven into the curatorial signature that defined each letter she composed to her sons. Her personal experience of tumultuous Yugoslav history, spanning the prewar period of the Kingdom of Yugoslavia and the postwar socialist period, followed by war again in the 1990s, created Gordana's sharp view of the actors and events that she, in turn, shared with her adult sons abroad. *Respect the country that opened its doors to you, but never forget where you came from*, pleaded Gordana with her sons. Because if the sons forgot where they came from, their mother's history would be lost as well. The meticulous letters that she wrote every day for years were a reminder to Vanja about his roots: "I try to keep him [Vanja] aware that he is Serb. Not a Serb nationalist in America, but a cosmopolitan who doesn't forget his origins. I think that is the worst: if you emigrate and forget who you are. My son cannot become an American after fifteen years spent there, like someone whose roots have been there for a hundred years. You will be unhappy then. This way you know that you have your homeland, your language, your alphabet, your friends; you have to preserve all that. You won't feel lost then."

Once again, Gordana drifted back to her own experience of migration while living in Macedonia to explain why awareness about one's roots mattered so much: "I was feeling lost in Macedonia; very far away from my place. There were no Serbs there. Some assimilated totally, but I didn't want that. I wanted to live there, to respect others, not to get into conflict with anyone. Even today I keep in touch with my ex-colleagues. I was friendly with everyone, I didn't emphasize my Serbianness, but I wanted to stay who I was. And I want my children to be who they are. Vanja has the full picture of the situation in Serbia. He knows both good and bad things going on here."

Throughout our encounter, Gordana spoke of both her sons and their migration journeys, but the letter she was writing at that time was for one son only. Gordana did not hide that she had a much better relationship with Vanja than her older son. They regularly kept in contact, mainly through letters and Vanja's weekly phone calls. The intimacy in her relationship with Igor seemed to have withered gradually over the years, whereas that with Vanja continued to thrive despite the distance between them. However, this had happened for a reason, as Gordana explained. According to

Gordana, she always had a different relationship with Igor. He was very hard working and always excelled at school; as a schoolboy, they sent him to summer school in England to learn the language. When he got a scholarship for a PhD in the United States, Gordana was not surprised. She knew he would want to go further in his career. In the early days of his migration, Gordana recalled, Igor wrote about the courses he was taking at the university and about his grades. He did not say much about his life in America. Gordana probed him with questions in her letters, asking him about life outside school, his friends, what he did other than study, and so on, but she did not get far. She knew that he was doing doctoral studies, that he had a scholarship, and that he had no financial problems—that was all. She had no idea about his life in the States. Maybe, she said, this was where her misunderstanding with Igor had begun. Unlike Igor, Vanja would write her about everything—about the prices of milk and bread, about the people he was hanging around with, about people from Belgrade that he met overseas, about parties and trips—giving his mother a colorful picture of his life and his experience of migration. "With Igor, it was more official, and I could never really get through to him or learn how he really was and what was really going on. And so we grew apart. I can't blame him or me for that, but we don't have such a good relationship. It is okay, we do communicate, but still, something is missing there. I was prepared when Igor left. But then everything crashed on me: my husband died, I moved to Belgrade, the war started, and then Vanja left."

While she had always known that Igor would leave Yugoslavia because he was gifted and ambitious, Vanja's departure was a shock. She never thought that Vanja would leave the country or go on to pursue a postgraduate degree in Canada some years later, as he had taken his time to finish his civil engineering degree in Belgrade. Unlike his older brother, Vanja was too much of a social butterfly to focus on his studies, said Gordana, adding, a bit tongue in cheek, "If his late father knew he would earn a master's degree in engineering one day, he would have turned around in his grave!"

Gordana's face lit up and a mischievous spark glinted in her eyes as she started to recount Vanja's dramatic departure to America. The level of detail in this mother's account pointed to the effect her younger son's migration had left on her, etched in her memory as if in stone. In July 1991, Gordana's husband died. At the time, Vanja was living with his wife in Banja Luka. Yugoslavia had started unraveling that summer, and Vanja was afraid of the military draft in Bosnia. To escape the draft, Vanja registered with the police and the army corps in Macedonia on the basis that he had been born and grew up there and that his late father was Macedonian. At the same time, Vanja's wife, an ambitious medical doctor, had won a scholarship for a postgraduate degree in medicine in the United States. Naturally, added Gordana, Vanja and his wife saw this as a lifeboat in which to escape the sinking ship and immediately bought tickets for New York. Her older son, Igor, arranged to meet them at the airport when they landed. Everything was going as planned until Vanja and his wife arrived at the Belgrade airport. They were about to board the plane when a police officer stopped him. A new law had just been passed, the police officer explained to Vanja, banning men between the ages of eighteen and sixty-five from leaving the country because of the compulsory military draft. The fact that he was registered with the Macedonian army sector did not matter. He was not allowed to leave the country. But this did not unnerve Vanja, Gordana said with glee: "Quick-witted as he was, Vanja told his wife to board the plane and promised to meet her in New York. At that time Macedonia was still a part of Yugoslavia and flights to Skoplje were classed as domestic air traffic. Before you knew it, Vanja was on a plane to Skoplje, where he arranged for a cousin to meet him. The cousin gave Vanja a lift by car to the Greek border, where they persuaded the policeman to let him across. They then carried on to the Thessaloniki airport, where Vanja caught the first plane to New York. Shortly after, he flew over Belgrade, leaving this country for good."

The events that she described had taken place fifteen years earlier, yet Gordana recalled every detail. It was a story she never wanted to forget. And although she did not hide the shock caused by her son's sudden departure shortly after her husband's death and her subsequent move from Macedonia to Serbia, Gordana delighted in her son's shrewdness. There was unmistakable cheerfulness in her voice and eyes as she recounted the story about Vanja's escape. She reveled in his prowess and disarming charm that had helped him find a way out of the country. Vanja's sudden emigration may have caused her pain, but more than this, Gordana was very proud of her son's clever escape from the coming military draft. Gordana's example was typical of all the mothers of conscription evaders whom I met during my fieldwork. Mothers were sad because they could not see their sons for years, but they had no remorse about encouraging or helping them to escape the military draft and leave the country.

According to the findings of Aleksandra Sasha Milićević's study about draft dodgers in Serbia, there was a stigma attached to those who escaped the army in the 1990s.[7] They were often portrayed as lesser men who were hiding under their mothers' skirts, labeled as "faggots" and "scumbags."[8] The prevailing nationalistic sentiment in the public discourse of the 1990s left no space for voices of mothers like Gordana. For years they carried their sorrow hidden from everyone. Gordana used to walk along the Danube early in the morning with a group of mothers from the area. With one exception, all of them had sons who had fled the country in the early 1990s, escaping the war and the crumbling of Yugoslavia. Strangers at first, they gradually went from polite nods to greetings until they finally started to walk together. Drawn together by a wish to find solace in long walks along the river, these mothers found comfort in each other's company, sharing their implicit understanding and experience. While these walks brought a brief respite in the wake of their sons' departure, their effects faded in comparison to the public silence and condemnation that surrounded much of the emigration in the 1990s.

The dominant public discourse of that time proscribed the draft dodgers for their lack of patriotism and for not being "manly" enough, as documented by Milićević.[9] Svetlana Slapšak captures some of that sentiment and the silence that fell on the older women who took part in helping draft dodgers escape the country in her much-acclaimed novel *Ravnoteža* [Equilibrium].[10] From hiding young men from military police to facilitating their emigration in the 1990s, older women did so in an attempt to save lives because they knew what war was and how irreversible its consequences were. Gordana's harrowing experience in a Croatian concentration camp in World War II has continued to haunt her. She loved her son and her homeland, Bosnia, too much to wish him to go to war there. In the 1990s, her anger and despair at seeing her beloved Bosnia butchered once more in her lifetime pushed Gordana to mine incessantly for more writings to share with her son. She wanted Vanja to understand what went on there, to read through politicians' motives and actions, to piece together this intricate puzzle with the help of her insight. During her visit to Vanja in Canada, Gordana found a French translation of a poem by Radovan Karadžić published in a Canadian magazine.[11] Gordana was outraged by it and had to share it with Vanja. She was emotional as she showed it to me:

> Karadžić wrote that poem before 1991 and look what he says there—can you imagine!—'[Let's go] to the city to kill the pests!' Can you imagine that? To kill the pests in the city!? Can you imagine—us in the city, we are the pests! And he was a psychiatrist, that man [pause]; and then he also says, 'I was born to

have no grave. This body was not born to smell flowers but to burn, kill, and turn everything into dust.' That is morbid, and so is everything that man has done [in Bosnia], I see him through those words . . . so yes, I collect these things and give them to my sons to read. I wasn't prepared for both sons to emigrate.

Perhaps the rapid succession of life-changing events is what made it so difficult for Gordana to come to terms with Vanja's migration: her husband's death, the outbreak of war in Yugoslavia, her departure from Macedonia where she had lived for more than thirty years, moving to a tiny apartment in Belgrade away from her friends in Macedonia and from both her sons. It is not surprising that her ritual letter writing to Vanja, embellished with thick descriptions of everyday life and the changes she witnessed as Yugoslavia crumbled, became so significant. Aside from book excerpts, news, and history, Gordana also shared updates about her neighbors. Vanja knew Gordana's neighbors because he had lived in the same building as a student in the 1980s. Gordana and her husband had bought a studio apartment in Belgrade in the 1970s for their sons to live in when they went to the university. Vanja was much liked by his neighbors; he was friendly, always smiling, and interested in the residents and the social life of the building. Even when he moved overseas, his mother kept him up to date with his former neighbors' lives. He was genuinely concerned, noted Gordana, when she wrote to him about a neighbor who had had heart surgery.

Gordana also included, in her cursive Cyrillic, some Bosnian expressions that were not common in Serbia but that she said reminded her of her youth and touched her heart. It should be pointed out that Gordana was aware that these letters mattered to her as much as she wanted her son to read them. She was reminding herself of her youth and life in Bosnia, a memory that she felt compelled to hold on to even more strongly in light of the destruction and suffering that had happened there again in the 1990s. A Bosnian Serb, she had lived most of her life outside Bosnia, first as a refugee in Serbia, then as a university student, then as an internal migrant in Macedonia with her husband where she raised her children. She was the Other in both Serbia and Macedonia, even though both republics were part of socialist Yugoslavia. Self-admittedly, she could have assimilated as other Serbs did in Macedonia, but she chose not to and held on to her identity. Gordana's actions affirm the argument that "the past takes a particularly prominent role in times of mobility and biographical rupture."[12]

Gordana's migration experience did not end in Macedonia. After her husband's death in 1991, Gordana left Macedonia and relocated to Serbia once again. Leaving the family home of thirty years in Macedonia, she moved into the small studio apartment in Belgrade where her sons had previously lived as students. She apologetically pointed to the furniture around her, noting that if she had known that she would live there for so long, she would have arranged the apartment more appropriately. In her view, nothing matched and it looked like she had just moved in. Gordana had left behind most of the furniture from their Macedonian home because it was too bulky for a small apartment in Belgrade and also because it reminded her of her husband. "The wardrobe and even the telephone smelled of my late husband for a long time," Gordana noted poignantly. But despite this matter-of-fact acceptance of her circumstances, an almost palpable sadness seeped through Gordana's narrative when she continued:

> I lived for thirty-two years in ninety square meters, and while it was nothing luxurious, it was a functional and tasteful space. I couldn't imagine that I would spend the next fifteen years alone in fifteen square meters. My whole life was spent there. I may seem depressed now, but I try not to show this to Vanja. I want him to think I am in a good mood. This whole situation—the war and the collapse of the state—all that lasted too long. You can't make any plans when the war is going on because you don't know what will happen tomorrow and if there will be any tomorrow. But still, I say thank God my children didn't go to war. We have seen a lot of everything, and not even today is the situation in Serbia as it should be. Somehow we as Serbs are at a loss. When you say that you are a Serb, it means you didn't manage to keep your state. You're someone who lost everything. Children should always be under their mother's wing. And as a Serb, you feel like an orphan, abandoned by everyone. You are left with nothing but sorrow.

There is a powerful metaphor here about a nation-state and a mother-child relationship and the grief of a nation deserted by its citizens and a mother abandoned by her child. This is an excellent example of how collective memory intertwines with personal memories, and vice versa. A personal experience of deportation to a concentration camp during World War II followed by a lifetime of migration in socialist Yugoslavia is woven into historical events from World War II, Yugoslavia, and its disintegration followed by a massive flow of refugees and migrants both into and out of the country. This becomes one memory in Gordana's narrative, rendering it impossible to discern whether she grieves for her migrant son(s), whom she was not able to keep by her side and thus feels that she failed as a mother, or whether she grieves for the Serbs in Bosnia who, because they allowed an unruly psychiatrist to lead them into a shameful war, have ended up as orphans, abandoned by mother Serbia and by everyone else. Gordana's experience of motherhood and her relationship with her sons thus becomes inextricably linked to a collective memory of being a Bosnian Serb. When she then passes that memory on to her son, it becomes impossible to tell whether that memory is her own, that of her family, or that of Bosnian Serbs. In the end, what matters is that one "cannot really run away from sorrow," as expressed in Ćopić's poem—be it as a mother of a migrant, as a refugee from a concentration camp, or as a Bosnian Serb. The sorrow is ingrained in them wherever they move.

Maurice Halbwachs introduced links between personal, family, and collective memory. In Gordana's case, we see how her relationship with her son(s) is directly related to her memories or, in fact, how her memories have shaped her relationship with her children.[13] In particular, Vanja's migration elicited her own very vivid memories of migration and the hardships she had to endure in various stages of that long migration itinerary. However, her memories were not only petrified memorials of times past. Gordana's memories also engaged with the 1990s war in Yugoslavia as well as with the migration of her sons, thus spanning and re-creating the past, present, and future.

Memories link the past, present, and future through the materiality of objects, which functions on the level of collective memory.[14] Regarding personal memory, elicitation is not necessarily embedded in material objects but, as seen throughout this book, is often embodied in one's children. For Belgrade mothers, migrant children are objectified memories of their motherhood and the events that surrounded it. The migration of their children caused a rupture in mothers' identity, triggering different strategies to restore a sense of wholeness.[15] The study of Belgrade mothers, however, lends evidence to indicate that migration disrupts the identities of mothers left behind as much as those of the migrants themselves.

Gordana's meticulous letter writing, embellished with excerpts from novels, poems, history, and news, was her way of reclaiming the identity doubly fractured by her and her sons' migration. Vanja did not grow up in Bosnia but Macedonia, so Gordana's use of Bosnian expressions in her letters was there not only to remind her son of his roots but also to remind herself of who she was. The excerpts from novels by Singer, Borges, and others spoke to her son's experience as a migrant as much as to her own. Gordana used her memories and her lifelong experience of being a refugee, a returnee, and a migrant to pass on her memories to her children without any reprimand or regret but with the stoic wisdom of a person who has seen and experienced enough to be wise, not to judge or hate. All that was left—and what she wanted her son to know in terms of her feelings about a lifelong migration journey from Bosnia—was sadness; thus, she insisted on copying the poem by Ćopić in a letter for her son. While she carefully guarded her feelings from Vanja and did not want him to see how she really felt because she did not want him to worry about her, trying to sound cheerful with him on the phone, Gordana channeled her emotions and experiences into the letters she wrote daily. This meticulous letter writing was more than just keeping in touch with her migrant sons. Gordana found vicarious atonement in her sons' migration that opened a new wound while simultaneously healing old ones: memories of injustice suffered as a girl in a concentration camp while strip-searched by her schoolteacher; of hardship as a refugee in occupied Serbia during World War II; of hope, happiness, and disappointment as a returnee to Bosnia after the war; of a life lived in friendly but foreign Macedonia and Serbia; and of the horrendous pain from seeing Bosnia torn apart yet again in the twilight of her life.

Just like the poem that she sent to Vanja, it seemed that indeed Bosnia haunted Gordana as well—she could not run away from sorrow. Gordana passed away in 2013. Vanja sent her on another, final journey back to Bosnia, where she was buried alongside her parents. Her lifetime of different migration routes and displacement took Gordana full circle back to her roots and to her much loved and longed-for Bosnia.

Notes

1. Gordana, interview by author, Belgrade, May 12, 2006.
2. Branko Ćopić originally published "Odgovor zemljaku" in a collection of poems entitled *Ratnikovo proljeće* [Warrior's spring] in 1945. Gordana chose to read the first two and last stanza from this eleven-stanza poem to me. I recorded them from her reading in Serbian and translated them into English. The original three stanzas are as follows:

> I drug mi priđe, odavna znan, mio
> i prijekor—pelin kao kamen pao:
> "Eh, ti nas, bogme, već zaboravio
> I ti—iz Bosne pobjegao!"

> O, moj Šefkete, dobričino stara,
> Kada ti tako, sta će drugi reći?
> Pa zar i tebe srce-oko vara?
> I zar se može od tuge pobjeći?
> . . .

Bosna i danas vodi moju ruku,
A to o bjekstvu—nemoj više reći,
I kad se ode, stare staze vuku.
A zar se može od tuge pobjeći?
[1945]

3. Jorge Luis Borges (1899–1986) was an Argentinian writer.

4. Queen Marija of Yugoslavia was the queen consort of King Aleksandar I of Yugoslavia. After the king was assassinated during a state visit to France in 1934, her oldest son, Petar II, eleven years old at the time, became the last king of Yugoslavia, while Marija became the Yugoslav queen mother (Jelavich, *History of the Balkans*). On March 25, 1941, the government of Prince Pavle (regent of the Kingdom of Yugoslavia) signed the Tripartite Pact, joining the Axis powers after being surrounded by Nazi allies from all sides. An uprising and massive demonstrations in Belgrade followed on March 27, along with a military coup d'état. As a consequence, the Nazi Luftwaffe bombed Belgrade on April 6 in Operation Punishment (*Unternehmen Strafgericht*), killing more than seventeen thousand civilians and destroying the National Library of Serbia and priceless medieval manuscripts, as well the Belgrade Zoo and all its animals. Immediately after the bombardments, Yugoslavia was occupied by Germans, Italians, Hungarians, and Bulgarians (Ibid.; Glenny, *The Balkans*).

5. NDH was established in April 1941 as a puppet state of Nazi Germany and Fascist Italy, which trained its military forces. It encompassed most of today's Croatia, the whole of today's Bosnia-Herzegovina, and parts of Slovenia and Serbia. Its population was around 6 million people, of whom 3 million were Croats, 2 million were Serbs, 750,000 were Bosnian Muslims, and the rest were Roma, Jews, and other minorities. The NDH aimed to become ethnically clean from Serbs, Jews, and Roma peoples. Under NDH rule, the entire Jewish population and around 700,000 Serbs were exterminated in the Jasenovac concentration camp in Croatia (Jelavich, *History of the Balkans*; Glenny, *The Balkans*).

6. Isaac Bashevis Singer (1902–91) was a Polish American writer and winner of the Nobel prize for literature in 1978.

7. Milićević, "Joining the War."

8. Ibid., 281.

9. Ibid.

10. Slapšak, *Ravnoteža*.

11. Radovan Karadžić, originally from Montenegro, became one of the leading figures among Bosnian Serbs, serving as the president of Republika Srpska during the war in Bosnia-Herzegovina in the 1990s. In March 2016, the International Crime Tribunal for the former Yugoslavia (ICTY) convicted Karadžić for war crimes and sentenced him to forty years' imprisonment.

12. Palmberger and Tošić, "Introduction," 1.

13. Halbwachs, *Collective Memory*.

14. Rowlands, "The Role of Memory," 144.

15. Sutton, *Remembrance of Repasts*.

6

FAMILY REVISITED

The Consequences of Migration

VLADIMIR, A MIDDLE-AGED ARCHITECT-TURNED-BICYCLE COURIER, WAS ONE OF the few London research participants who agreed to put me in touch with family in Serbia. I met Vladimir through an English friend who had lived with him for a while in East London. Vladimir, who arrived in London in 1992, had not been back to Serbia when I met him in 2005. His parents and sister were still living in Serbia, and although they had not seen each other for many years, Vladimir and his family kept in touch.

When I went to Belgrade in spring 2006, I contacted Vladimir's mother, Anka, for an interview. She agreed immediately but asked me to wait for a few weeks because she wanted me to meet her daughter as well and needed time to arrange a meeting between the three of us. Anka and her husband, in their late sixties and early seventies, lived in a small town near Belgrade. She was a retired teacher, and he was a retired engineer. After Vladimir left the country in the early 1990s, their daughter, Jelena, moved into his apartment in Belgrade, and we arranged to meet there.

Anka was waiting for me in the hallway outside the apartment at the elevator doors.[1] She smiled and looked at me closely, as if she had not seen me for a while, although we had never met. She ushered me into the apartment, and as I entered, I met her daughter, Jelena, who was sitting in the living room.[2] The three of us sat around a small table, and as I prepared for the interview and set my notebook and pencil on the table, I heard Anka suddenly begin to weep. Her daughter lowered her head.

A heavy silence fell on us until Anka stuttered through tears, "What can I tell you about my Vladimir? I haven't seen him for fifteen years."[3] As much as Anka's tears spoke of her emotions, her daughter's silence and bowed head conveyed her feelings as well. They both seemed to be in profound grief, and my visit had clearly disturbed them. We had gathered in the absent son's apartment to talk about him, and during those long minutes of weeping, his absence was more tangible than anything else in the room. The pain of his absence made his mother break down in front of a stranger who had come to interview her; it made his sister turn silent and still. The absent son was an invisible conductor standing in the room and orchestrating this eruption of emotions.

After a while, Anka gathered herself and started to talk about her son. She believed he worked so hard for sheer survival that he could not afford to come and visit them. She did not want to be a burden to him and offered to come to London with a tourist agency so that he would not have obligations toward her, promising they would only meet whenever it was convenient for him. However, Vladimir told her not to come, promising he would come to visit them instead. It had been like that for fifteen years, said Anka. Her feelings drifted from sadness to anger to despair to hope and back to sadness again:

> God knows how many times I said I would go to see him, regardless of whether he wants it or not. And then again, I think, what's the point in going there against his will? What if he would get angry and say, 'Mother, why did you come here? We didn't agree on this.' My friends keep asking me, 'How do you manage not to see Vladimir for so many years?' And I say, 'I have to. I don't have a choice.' It was much harder in the beginning; now as the years are passing, it is still hard, of course, but now I dream that the door will open; while I'm sitting here, Vladimir will show up, walk in to surprise me. This is my dream now. I would still like it to happen, but it will be as God says. It is all God's will. I am seventy, I approach the end of life, and I have witnessed that [it is all God's will]. I say to our closest friends that Vladimir doesn't call, and to others, I say that he calls. I didn't give birth to him to be separated from him for so many years. I thought he would live in our country and that everything would be all right. But it wasn't. That wretched war and everything that was going on here . . . horror. Also, the bombings in 1999, [pause] as if it were a dream.

Anka fell silent for a moment, as if she were searching for words to explain her son's absence:

> He became estranged. I am not sure that it is just because he works a lot that he can't visit us. It seems that he accepted that world of alienation and that he doesn't need us any longer. The only thing left is when I tell him at the end of our conversation, 'Your mother kisses you,' and he replies, 'I kiss you too, Mother.' We write to each other [emails] on the internet, and every time I try to say some gentle words, he would make fun of it—I guess that's his way of

pushing away nostalgia and of letting me know that he is not so sad about not being with us. He used to be very sensitive, very emotional. I think that the severity of the tense and challenging life over there has made him stronger and more robust. However, I also feel that he is a coward and that he is afraid not so much of the meeting as much as of the separation, how he will survive that.

I let the interview digress and tried not to interrupt Anka's narrative too much. I wanted to learn from her how she made sense of her son's absence without (mis)leading her answers with my questions. From the first few sentences, it was immediately clear that Anka was gravely wounded and that she had suffered for years. Even when she offered to come to London with a tourist agency to see him, Vladimir talked her out of it. When his promises to visit her had not materialized for fifteen years, Anka resigned her hope to God. The idea that Vladimir would walk through the door one day became a dream, supplanting the nightmare of the 1990s wars.

Throughout our conversation, Anka kept slipping into the past. She was much more comfortable talking about her son in the past tense: what he was like as a boy, what he used to do as a teenager, how charming and handsome he was, and how all the neighbors used to tell her that she had the most beautiful boy in the whole town. Every time she touched on his life in London in her narrative, Anka became uncomfortable and apologetic:

> The two of us are alike: easygoing, light-spirited, optimists. However, he somehow became much more serious. He had a severe knee injury, and he was mistreated at the university there, but he never wanted to talk to us about all that. We don't even know if he finished his studies because he won't talk to us; we don't know what he's doing. He says, 'I construct and work a lot.' So sometimes when I ask him what he's doing, he says, 'I'm chasing my tail.' I only laugh at that. Some old friend of his told us that he finished a master's in architecture, but he never said anything. [pause] There is something else there as well. You know, Vladimir was very handsome and beautiful, and I fear that maybe now that he has gotten older his hair has become gray and perhaps he is bald, and that's why he wouldn't send us any photos. When I ask him to send us a picture, he only sends some where you can see his profile or something like that. So, either something happened with him, or he is so vain that he doesn't want us to see how he looks nowadays. Well, he is forty-three, you know.

Anka suddenly stopped and gave me a long, silent look. Even though she did not say it aloud, one could feel the heaviness of her question hanging in the air. As I sat listening and watching the despair of a mother longing to see her son, I found myself in an awkward position. I knew how her son looked, where he lived, what he ate; I knew his girlfriend, some of his friends; I knew what he did for a living, and I knew that he would not go to Serbia because he did not want to. I even had Vladimir's photo, and photos of his house, on my camera sitting in a bag on the floor next to me. I sat there, torn between my ethical obligations toward the son and the pressing need to answer the mother's unasked question about her estranged son, carefully weighing how to resolve this dilemma. Finally, I decided to tell this mother what she hoped to hear about her son: that he was busy, that he worked hard—intimating that was probably the reason he could not visit them—and that he looked excellent for his age. I do not know if this makes me a lesser anthropologist, but I felt that it was the right thing to do.

Reassured by my words about her son, Anka drifted back to the safe territory of his childhood. She showed me photos of Vladimir and his sister, Jelena, when they were seven and eight; a picture of Vladimir during his military service when he was eighteen; the four of them as a family. Anka pointed out Vladimir and Jelena's father in a photo, noting that he was seventy-one and adding that Vladimir looked youthful like his father. Suddenly, she changed the subject, asking if I knew that Vladimir had a son. As I had not known about this, Anka explained that Miljan was born two weeks before Vladimir left the country. Miljan's mother did not initially want to see them after Vladimir had abandoned her and the baby. Since his first birthday, however, Anka and her husband had been in touch regularly with their only grandson and his mother:

> He [Miljan] adores his grandfather, and he loves going with him to the summer house in the hills. We accepted him as our grandson, even though Vladimir, his father, rejected him. Miljan wanted to meet his father, and last year his mother took him to London to meet Vladimir. What I didn't like was that when Miljan reached out to kiss his father, Vladimir moved away and offered to shake hands instead. That really hurt me. I can understand that the boy wasn't growing up next to him, but if he reached out to him, Vladimir should have at least hugged him.

Anka's regret over her son's lack of emotional display for the son he disavowed many years ago was quite apparent. Miljan had noticed that Vladimir had no bed—he slept on the floor. Even though he described this to his grandmother as an unpleasant surprise, after a while, Miljan boasted that he too had started sleeping on the floor. Anka took this as a sign that Miljan would like to get closer to Vladimir by copying him, and she tried to steer him toward the good things that her son used to do. However, she hastily added that she was afraid her son's behavior would hurt her grandson because he would not invite Miljan to visit him in London. Accustomed to this cold treatment from her son, Anka comforted her grandson with the same words she used to console herself:

> I told Miljan that Vladimir would invite him but that he's got his hands full—he works all day and wouldn't have time to be with him, that's why he's not calling him. You know, the boy wouldn't stay there long. He would be there three or four days, no longer, and that would make him happy. I am sorry that he is not thinking about the boy's future; he should think about how that boy is feeling. Miljan was growing up next to us, and we didn't reject him. Vladimir keeps his son's photo in his apartment in England and some friends of his who visited him told us, 'Oh, we know Miljan, we've seen his photo.' However, he did not grow up next to him, and there you go. . . . What can I do?

Anka candidly admitted that she wanted to learn more about Vladimir from her grandson, who had had a chance to see him. She probed Miljan about Vladimir's looks, and he confirmed that Vladimir was still good-looking. That was not enough for her, and she asked Miljan how tall he was next to Vladimir. Miljan's affirmative reply, that Vladimir was very tall next to him, prompted another question from Anka, as if with each answer she came a bit closer to seeing her son through her grandson's eyes. Anka relayed a conversation she had with her grandson after his visit to meet his father:

> "And what is he like? Has he gone gray?" asked Anka.
> "Well, no, Granny—he has beautiful hair; maybe he colors it, but he has very few gray hairs. You know, he is handsome," Miljan reassured his grandmother.
> However, this was still not enough, so Anka repeated once again, "Is he handsome?"
> "Yes, he is handsome," Miljan confirmed. "And," he added, "he was wearing a T-shirt that he made himself."

Vladimir, explained Anka to me, had loved sewing ever since he was in primary school: "He made shirts and . . . everything! He would sit at the machine and *rrrm, rrrm, rrrm*. I bought a new Bagat [sewing machine], and when I saw him at it, I had a nervous breakdown. He would repair his jeans, make shirts, trousers, coats, everything . . . [pause] He was funny."

Her grandson's description of Vladimir and his passing remark about a T-shirt transported Anka back to her son's childhood. Anka might have been upset with her son at the time for using her brand-new sewing machine without asking, but she took pride in his ideas and creations.

Anka continued providing details from Vladimir's childhood: how he liked to polish his shoes or how he loved painting and used to spill the water from the paintbrushes all around the house. She recalled that Vladimir liked to keep his room tidy, and how, when she would go into his bedroom during the night to put his clothes on a chair, he would get angry because she had put them in a different order from his. He preferred staying at home during the summer holidays instead of going to the seaside and spent whole summers at his grandmother's house, painting and doing all sorts of creative things.

Throughout our conversation, Anka drifted back into the past and reminisced about her son in the past tense. The story about Miljan came up in our chat about Vladimir's youthful looks, which Miljan had inherited from his father together with his blue eyes and dark hair. The presence of the rejected grandson, Miljan, objectified the absence of the departed son in London. Not only did Miljan elicit memories of her estranged son because of his physical resemblance and by way of his presence in Anka's home, but the role of the grandson in Anka's view was also to elicit her son's memories of his forsaken family in Serbia. The latter, however, did not happen, and Anka was appalled to hear from Miljan that his father—her son—kept himself at a distance and refused to show any emotion toward his own son. Unsurprisingly, Anka found it easier to petrify a memory of her son as a child and continually slipped into the past during our conversation.

While the mother talked about the absent son, his sister, Jelena, sat next to us looking even more absent than her brother in London. I asked Jelena about her contact with Vladimir, whether the two of them kept in touch, and how that had changed over the years. Jelena recalled that he was more active in communicating during the first half of the 1990s. The breaking point, in Jelena's view, happened in 1998 when her brother got indefinite leave to remain (ILR) in the United Kingdom.[4] Until then, he could not leave the country. But even though he was allowed to leave the United Kingdom after receiving the ILR, Vladimir did not come when Jelena asked him to visit them. Unlike her mother, however, Jelena was not trying to find excuses for her brother.

> **Jelena:** I think that his perceptions are different from ours. The same way we now have the impression that he has forgotten us, I think that his impression that we have forgotten him is even stronger . . . because [pause] it is true, [pause] it is true that the one who is not here, you can do without him. Even though I am not his mother, it is different for the

one who leaves than for the one who stays and may or may not write but cannot understand what's going on there . . . [pause] I think [pause] that those who stay grow apart more than those who go away [pause] in some way. Because they are in a new and different environment and you can't imagine how all that looks and feels. Maybe he expects that we should look after him and worry about him more because he is away . . . [pause] maybe even write six times for every single time that he writes to us.

Anka interrupted Jelena: I was writing to him every single week. And he wouldn't write back for two or three months. And we didn't know anything about him. No, we knew nothing about him. . . .

Jelena: And maybe it was easier for him to cut us off like that. . . .

Anka: Only when he was working in that office, he used to tell us it was all right there and that he liked it there; or when he had an argument with some professor at the university, he told us about that as well. Those were all episodes . . . [pause] some snippets from his life . . . [pause] but no, nothing more than that.

Jelena: It was only last fall that he wrote to me about how he had serious crises there and that he resolved them fairly recently. I assume it was related to nostalgia. He used to write before . . . [pause] before, we were more in touch; fair enough, I never wrote to him, but I used to phone him. On one occasion I spent all my salary on the phone bill. Whole salary! [She laughs.] They cut off my phone, and I went to the phone company to check what happened, and I saw that there was that huge bill to pay. . . . [pause] I had just received my salary that day, and I withdrew everything I had from the bank to pay that phone bill. Okay, those were the 1990s when salaries were miserably low, but still, it was my entire monthly income that I gave for the phone bill. . . . So yes, we did keep in touch up until some point. . . . [pause] He used to say to me, 'Do you know what it's like when you wake up under the foreign sky? Until I've had my coffee and a cigarette, I can't do anything.' However, he was never more specific what it was about, if it was nostalgia or family or whatever . . . we don't go too deep into any emotional subject; when it becomes too deep, we stop writing.

Following a long silence, Anka took over the conversation from her daughter once again, saying she was mostly in contact with him and wrote him lengthy emails. Vladimir, said Anka, would not reply for a long time. He would then apologize, saying that he was busy, and would write no more than a few sentences. Anka wrote extensively about the whole family (*familija*),[5] where each of them was living at the time, how they were, and what they did in life. According to Anka, however, Vladimir was not interested in even his closest relatives. Sometimes he inquired about Anka's aunt, with whom he had been very close since childhood. The aunt was ninety in 2006, and Vladimir occasionally asked how "Granny" was doing, so Anka wrote to him about Granny, as she was the only one who interested him. He asked about his father—how Dad was doing, if he had gone to the summer house—but that was it, said Anka; he was not in touch with anyone in the family. He did not write to them, nor did they call him:

> So, he exists in theory but practically he has been erased here. He has lots of cousins, but no one would ever call him. I told them it's cheaper for them to call him than for him to call all of them, but they wouldn't listen. It's only us two, mother and father, who still keep in touch with him. I write to him, and then I get angry because he doesn't reply for a long time, and I say I will never do it again. And then after some time I write again even though I said I wouldn't. He then says, 'Forgive me, Mother,' or 'Mom,' and I like when he calls me 'Mother' . . . so I write to him again and again even though he seldom replies to my emails.

The difference between mother and sister in relation to their estranged son and brother could not have been more striking. While the mother was hurt and at times frustrated with his behavior, she was also forgiving and kept reaching out to him; the sister's reaction, however, was very different. Jelena had initially invested a lot of effort and occasionally made very substantial material sacrifices to stay in touch with him, such as spending her entire monthly salary on a phone call to her brother in London. However, her eagerness to keep in touch and preserve the intimacy in their relationship had gradually withered away as a consequence of Vladimir's continual failures to reciprocate. After several failed attempts to keep the relationship going, Jelena gave up and openly spoke of him as lost to the family. Unlike her mother, Jelena accepted that he was no longer part of her life just as she was no longer part of his and that they would never have the same relationship as before he left Serbia.

This contrast suggests that the relationship between siblings in 1990s and early 2000s Serbia was more similar to nonkin relationships than to a parent-child relationship, which was much more normative and remained so even in the context of migrant children. The relationship between migrant and nonmigrant siblings was based more on their relation to each other rather than on norms of what a relationship between a brother and a sister ought to be like. I came across a range of very different relationships between brothers and sisters, from very close ones to those in which individuals had lost almost all contact with each other, depending on the quality of the connection in the premigration period. In contrast, the parent-child relationship was dominated more by norms that dictated certain expectations about mothers' or fathers' roles toward their children.

During our conversation, Vladimir's father was barely mentioned. When I asked whether he had any contact with Vladimir, Anka said that their communication was "official."[6] That meant, Anka explained, that Vladimir would ask his father how he was, to which his father would respond with something about politics and the situation in Serbia. His father, according to Anka, did not ask his son what he was doing because he knew Vladimir would give him an evasive reply, and he found it easier not to ask Vladimir anything. Vladimir's father had been an engineer but, Anka pointed out, he did not know how to use the internet. Anka had learned how to use a computer and send emails because of Vladimir, as she felt it was the easiest way to keep in touch with her son. She had asked Jelena to show her what to do, writing everything down as she went. Her husband, Anka said, was too proud to ask anyone to show him how to use a computer. Instead, he chose to dictate his letters to Anka, who then sent them on his behalf. However, he did not write to Vladimir as much as to Miljan, who had recently moved abroad with his mother. He was very fond of Miljan and felt there was no point writing to Vladimir because he was an adult, whereas Miljan was still a child. Anka did not write down her husband's dictation word for word. She rephrased his wording and changed the style according to her taste. Her husband complained that it was not what he meant to say, but Anka persisted. "I have to give it some style!" Anka added with a hint of glee.[7] She then stopped there for a while, as if she were trying to find the right words for what she wanted to say next:

> He never had that parental, fatherly stance toward Vladimir. He was competitive and underestimated whatever Vladimir did. Today, he says, 'I am afraid that our Vladimir is the kind of man who lives for a day, that he is a bohemian and that he has wasted his life.' But I don't think so . . . [pause]; Vladimir does not drink alcohol. He does not smoke. He lives in his world. He always had his self-sufficient world, and he was different from other children. He could spend hours watching a column of ants walking along the ceiling in my aunt's house. Or he would go out to play soccer, and then when he'd had enough, he'd turn around and come home to do something else. He had his world back then and his plans. Today, he also has his world, his own life; this is how he chose to live, and he apparently can live without us.

This was one of my last interviews in Belgrade, and as I was soon returning to London, I offered to bring a parcel to Vladimir in case Anka wanted to send him something. I had volunteered the same to Vladimir before going to Belgrade, and he thanked me, saying there was nothing he wanted to send there and that he also did not need anything from there.

His mother asked if I could take two or three liters of *šljivovica*.[8] I agreed to take one liter, offering to bring something else like photographs, books, or some food. Anka shrugged her shoulders regretfully, saying that he did not eat "our" food anymore, not even sausages, because his tastes had changed:

> I know that he doesn't drink *šljivovica* either, but maybe his friends will like it, and I want him to have something from home to share with them. He always liked to gather friends, to cook, bake cakes . . . he was still in primary school when he would bring a bunch of school friends home and bake crepes for them. . . . [pause] I would only see the smoke coming out of the kitchen . . . then they would go to Jelena's room and make a mess there. . . . [pause] Yes, he always liked to cook. It was nothing for him to make rice pudding and bring a bunch of friends over to share it with them. He was a very social boy; he liked to play soccer, to hang around with his friends. . . . [pause] Though I think in love he was very emotional and vulnerable and he would get hurt after a breakup. So, he had that girlfriend, he fell out with her, Yugoslavia fell apart, the war started, and he went on the world tour with the theater he worked at . . . that was the last time we saw him.

As with Gordana's case in chapter 5, here we see how personal and family memories become enmeshed with collective memory, and thus the breakup of Yugoslavia becomes a pretext for Vladimir's split with his girlfriend and, in a way, with his family in Serbia. Thereby, when talking about the breakup of Yugoslavia, Anka would blame it for the loss of her son, who fled the country to escape the army draft, leaving not only Yugoslavia but his girlfriend and newborn son, his parents and sister, and the rest of his family. The only physical proof of his existence was Miljan, whom Vladimir's parents and family had thoroughly embraced as their grandson even though his father repudiated him. The grandson thus became an objectified memory of a lost son. If objects are carriers of collective memories and links between past, present, and future, this research shows that people—especially children—are the objectification of personal memories and connections to collective memories.[9]

For Anka, her son's departure and his fifteen-year absence were more comfortable to explain and accept if put into the framework of collective memories: she could thus say that her son had to leave because of the war and that he had not visited them because he could not afford it. Even though she occasionally allowed a shadow of doubt to fall over her explanation for her son's virtual disappearance from the family, Anka kept returning to her belief with the same zeal with which she kept sending him emails without receiving a reply. That zeal is also what compelled Anka to send a bottle of *šljivovica* to her son despite knowing that he did not drink or eat traditional Serbian food. With this gift, Anka sought to affirm that despite all the changes and estrangement her son was still the same as when he was a boy, and she hoped that he would invite friends around and share the drink with them. By doing so, he would attest to still being the son she knew.

What matters more than the actual son, seemingly, is the idea of a son in relation to a mother. In other words, mother-as-term and child-as-term are categories that come into being only through enacting their mutual relationship. There is no concept of the mother without an idea of the child, and vice versa.[10] In a mother-child relation where the son refuses to play his part, the absence of the person prepared to inhabit the category of son implies the absence of the mother as well. To mourn a missing son is also to mourn a missing mother. Thus, the somber atmosphere that characterized most of my encounters with mothers of migrant sons or daughters from Belgrade was not caused only by grief felt for a child who had gone away for good. It was as much a lament for one's loss of herself as a mother.

Negotiating Family Relationships

Sociological research in the 1990s and early 2000s suggests that family relationships in Serbia had a strong normative aspect.[11] It was customary, especially after the economic collapse in the 1990s, to find older people living with their children and grandchildren, as well as to find adult daughters looking after their own families and caring for their mothers(-in-law) and fathers(-in-law).[12] Until the early 1990s, most families in Serbia had been nuclear. With the disintegration of Yugoslavia and massive pauperization in the early 1990s, households started to expand to include several generations. As a result, almost half of all families in Serbia lived in collective households in the early 2000s.[13] Serbia had one of the oldest populations at that time but only nine thousand places in care homes for the elderly.[14] The first association of private care homes in Serbia was established in 2006, consisting of only six homes.[15] Daycare centers and clubs for the elderly were still just an idea in 2014, as there were numerous obstacles to expanding options of care for the elderly outside the privacy of home and family obligations.[16] In a situation where there were not nearly enough places for the elderly in care homes and where social expectations dictated that families should look after their elderly members, it was unsurprising to find that adult children were the primary providers of care for the elderly.

Almost two-thirds of households in Serbia in the early 2000s looked after an elderly live-in family member.[17]

Migration, however, profoundly affected family relationships. The distance and infrequent contact between migrants and families left behind increased the discrepancy between the normative ideals and expectations, on the one hand, and the actual person, on the other.[18] Mothers left behind, as we have seen throughout this book, showed tremendous resilience and developed special rituals in response to this discrepancy. Milena (see chapter 3) acted as a curator of family memories, carefully preserving objects and spaces that reminded her of people and the time when they lived together. Through embodied practices and rituals around her home, Milena created order and a sense of tranquility. In contrast, Mirjana (also from chapter 3) had no interest in keeping her grandchildren's photos around the home because she did not feel close to them. Mirjana took charge in dealing with a discrepancy between the normative and processual relationship with her son and his daughters, creating her own family through painstaking needlework.

While Mirjana's was an extreme case, the practices—more than words—of other mothers suggested that when faced with failed expectations in relationships with their children, women took active agency. Ana (see chapters 3 and 4) was very fond of her grandchildren and kept their photos displayed in a glass cabinet. However, she kept their recent photos tucked behind the ones that showed them as much younger children whom she had lived with and had memories of. Right next to them, Ana kept pictures of her lodger, who occupied a special place in her current life. Having not seen her son and grandchildren for ten years, Ana still loved them deeply, but the experience of a relationship with a child in her life, as someone she could care about and someone who was there for her as well, was negotiated instead with her boarder. Ana's son also broke normative expectations of a child; he had neither visited nor invited his mother to visit for over a decade since emigrating.

In contrast to both Ana's son and Anka's son, Vladimir, Gordana's younger son, Vanja, maintained a close relationship with his mother. Vanja played his role of a son—he showed interest in what she would write him about, invited her to visit him a few times, and kept her up to date with what happened in his life—and Gordana did the same as a mother. Vanja's older brother, Igor, however, did not play the same role of a son, and Gordana was aware of the difference between them. Both sides in this mother-child relationship retracted. Once again, we see in this example how cultural norms are negotiated depending on actual experience; once again, we see that mothers and their migrant children were not bound by cultural norms but instead each asserted their agency in the relationship, subverting the strong normative aspect of Serbian kinship.

Thus, while family relationships in the 1990s and early 2000s were still dominated by normative expectations from both parents and children, in the context of migration, there was more negotiating within this normative cultural frame.[19] Now I want to touch briefly on migrant women's own experience of motherhood. It was not uncommon for adult children—in particular, daughters—to evade cultural norms concerning their parents only to turn back to normative expectations in relationships with their own children. The following paragraphs highlight how migrant women's experience of motherhood affected family relationships.

In chapter 2, we met Ljubica, who had emigrated from Belgrade to London in the early 1990s. At the time of my London fieldwork in 2005, Ljubica was married, had a four-year-old girl, and was pregnant with a second child. Ljubica recounted that her experience of everyday life had changed when her daughter started going to a nursery. When she went to pick up her daughter from the nursery, Ljubica realized that she was a "foreign mother." While at work she was valued as an expert and her ethnic background was irrelevant; at the school gate, however, her different views on child raising made a big difference.

The experience of raising a child in the United Kingdom as directly related to a change in one's sense of belonging and subjectivity was a common theme among Serbian migrant women in my London research. Ljubica's case was typical of many other migrant mothers I met, for whom children objectified their otherness. Having a child is part of a woman's bodily experience, and such physical memories have a more profound and prolonged effect. From pregnancy to giving birth and raising a child, there were numerous differences in their new homeland that migrant women from Belgrade could not adapt to or accept because they clashed with their notions of what it meant to be a good mother: having only two scans (at twelve and twenty weeks) during pregnancy in the United Kingdom, delivering a baby without a doctor but only with a midwife, being instructed how they ought to feed a baby, to being told how to dress (or not to dress) a child—these were some of the issues raised by my female informants in London as incongruous with their culture. Thus, even though their ideas of what being a good daughter meant might have changed in comparison to such normative notions in Serbia, as mothers, they still perpetuated normative expectations of what it meant to be a good mother.

Ljubica gave birth to her second child toward the end of my fieldwork. Her parents promised to come and help out with the baby, as her husband had to work and Ljubica would be on her own with an older girl and a newborn. Ljubica's British husband considered it his right as a father to bathe the baby in the evening and disapproved of his mother-in-law interfering. Ljubica's mother, however, considered it inappropriate for a man to bathe a newborn baby and criticized her daughter for allowing her husband to interfere in what she thought to be a "woman's task." Ljubica tried to compromise but eventually had to ask her parents not to stay for the six months as planned but to leave after just three weeks. Although in need of their help, she found it even more draining trying to balance the expectations of her mother and her husband.

This example illustrates the incongruence between normative and processual kinship relations that can be contained in one person. Ljubica's mother did what mothers in Serbia were expected to do—she and her husband stayed with their daughter after she gave birth and looked after the baby while their daughter recovered. Ljubica's husband did what he felt was the right thing to do as a father, and he wanted to take responsibility for looking after their newborn baby. Ljubica, thus trapped between her role as a good daughter and a good wife, decided to break Serbian kinship norms and asked her parents to leave much earlier than they had planned. Had she been living in Serbia, this might not have happened, as gender norms are more prescriptive about men's presence around newborn babies and mothers. Traditionally, this has been an area reserved for older women, enabling them to exercise their power in family relationships and negotiate patriarchal patterns.[20] This does not preclude exceptions to the norm, as there are increasingly more fathers among the younger generations in Serbia who are more involved in the care and upbringing of their young children. But the prevailing norms still consider grandmothers to be the primary source of help when their daughters give birth.

In his study of shopping in North London, Daniel Miller argues that the anxieties and tensions that arise from a mother-child relationship stem from clashes between a mother's idealized image of her child and that of her real child.[21] The mothers in Miller's study would go shopping for food thinking of what would be best for their child to eat. When confronted with a child that does not necessarily want to eat what is healthy but rather what tastes good and what mothers often consider unhealthy, mothers would then try to find a compromising solution that would hopefully satisfy—at least to some extent—both the child and the mother. Miller argues that relationships and kinship are not relational (or processual or negotiated), as anthropologists and other social scientists have claimed.[22] He suggests that in dealing with relationships, we have to deal as much with the normative structure represented by kin categories as with any actual behavior of those who occupy these categories—a discrepancy that is very evident in this chapter.[23] The examples of Ljubica, Jelena, Ana, Gordana, and many other mothers and migrants in this book support Miller's call for a dialectical approach in kinship studies.[24] Ljubica's example, in particular, has highlighted the change in migrants' subjectivity through the experience of motherhood. However, another event that had a profoundly transformational influence on migrants' subjectivity and experience of family relationships was death.

The Transformative Power of Death

As mentioned earlier, several of my London research participants refused to put me in touch with their parents or family in Belgrade. The reason for this in several cases was the death of one of the parents or a sibling. My informants felt that my visit to family in Serbia would be disturbing and a painful reminder of a family member whom they had lost.

This was also the case with Ljubica, who was incredibly generous and forthcoming with my research in London but would not put me in touch with her parents in Belgrade. She was concerned that my visit and conversation with her parents about their relationship with migrant children might be distressing, as it would remind them of their son, Nemanja, who had passed away a few years earlier. Ljubica had been very close to her brother. Nemanja and his wife had moved to Canada in the early 1990s as highly skilled migrants. After they had settled down, Nemanja's parents came to visit from Belgrade on tourist visas. A few years later, Nemanja initiated the procedure for becoming a sponsor for his parents so that they could visit him without having to go through the expensive and tiring process of applying for a Canadian tourist visa each time. While his parents were preparing to visit him for the first time with their new sponsorship visas, Nemanja tragically lost his life. A few months later, his wife organized a memorial for her late husband in Toronto. Ljubica came from London, while her parents set off from Belgrade to attend the remembrance ceremony. When her parents arrived at the Toronto airport, they hit a brutal wall of bureaucracy: the immigration officer told them that they could not enter Canada because their sponsor was dead. They spent five hours at the Toronto airport immigration office explaining that they had only come to attend a memorial for their son, not to move to Canada. The parents waited all day for a reply from the immigration authorities to tell them whether they could attend their son's memorial. Eventually, the immigration authorities granted the parents permission to enter Canada for forty-eight hours only, and their sponsorship visas were annulled. Ljubica suffered greatly throughout this tragic situation. She was shocked to learn that she had no rights to even enquire about her brother following the accident in which he had lost his life. The information about her brother's death, Ljubica learned from relevant authorities, would only be discussed with his wife. The death of her brother pointed poignantly to essential differences in the conceptualization of kinship relationships and the rights one has over his or her relatives.

The transformative effect of death had a profound impact on Vladimir and his family too. In 2007, Vladimir went home for the first time after sixteen years to attend his sister Jelena's funeral. The emotions caused by his presence at the funeral were so strong that he decided to revisit his parents several months later. His mother, Anka, was crying in sorrow for her daughter one minute, then crying for joy at the sight of her son the next. It seemed that for the first time in sixteen years, Vladimir realized that he was still a part of the family and that his presence meant a lot to his parents, especially at such a difficult period.

Death had a transformative effect on families left behind as well. In summer 2008, Ljiljana's husband, Milutin (see chap. 3) suffered a severe stroke with devastating consequences. Taking into consideration his age (eighty-two) and the severity of the stroke, doctors said it was unlikely that he would recover and transferred him to a hospice outside Belgrade. He lingered for almost a whole month, during which time most of his family came to say goodbye. His condition progressively deteriorated, and it was evident that he would not recover. Milutin passed away in early June 2008. His son, Petar, did not come from the United States to say goodbye to his father during his last days, nor did he come to the funeral. Milutin's three younger sisters concluded that Petar was no longer part of the *familija* because not even his father's death was a strong enough reason for him to come from America, pay his father his last respects, and bury him as he was expected to do. In their view, Petar had not only wronged his late father but the whole family who had gathered together to mourn the loss of their eldest member.

Milutin was the oldest of four children and the only brother. Born to a patriarchal family that originated from Herzegovina, following his parents' death in the early 1980s, Milutin assumed the role of "bearer" of the family name and tradition. After their parents' death, the whole family—all his sisters and their families—gathered at Milutin's home to celebrate Christmas and the family *slava* (patrilineal family patron saint). Milutin was much older than his three sisters and acted as a father figure to them. He was also the most educated in the family, holding a doctorate in economics, and the most successful in his career, all of which contributed to accumulating prestige and authority among his extended family. His wife, daughter, and sisters all stood in the church next to the coffin to accept condolences from the extended family and friends who came to Milutin's funeral. During the procession of the casket from the chapel to the grave, the cross—usually carried by a son leading the procession—was carried instead by Milutin's eldest nephew. The absence of Milutin's son at his father's funeral and his absence from collective mourning with the rest of the family were disruptive for the extended family: this was not only Milutin's funeral but also the social death of his son. In everyday life in urban Serbia today, the *familija* (extended family) has limited influence over the *porodica* (nuclear family) and individual family members. However, when it comes to death, conservatism and the strict normative expectations of the extended family and collective take over. Even if one does not agree with Émile Durkheim's structural functionalism, it is still clear that death is generally seen as having both positive and negative aspects in the way that it is constitutive of relationships through mourning and through the normativity that underlies our relationship to relationships.[25]

Notes

An earlier version of this chapter was published in "Unmaking Family Relationships: Belgrade Mothers and Their Migrant Children," in *Anthropology and the Individual: A Material Culture Perspective*, ed. D. Miller (Oxford, UK: Berg, 2009), 115–30. The material is used by permission of Bloomsbury Publishing.

1. Anka, interview by author, Belgrade, June 29, 2006.

2. Jelena, interview by author, Belgrade, June 29, 2006.

3. Vladimir did not go straight from Belgrade to London but instead spent some time traveling with the theater company he used to work for. So while he had lived in London for fourteen years at that point, it had been fifteen years since he had departed from Belgrade.

4. Indefinite leave to remain (ILR) or permanent residency (PR) allows a migrant to reside permanently and to work in the United Kingdom.

5. In Serbia, the word *familija* refers to one's extended family, whereas *porodica* stands for the nuclear family; in this case, my interviewee referred to the extended family.

6. She used the term *zvaničan*, which can also mean "aloof" or "distant."

7. This example echoes Anđelka Milić's argument about Yugoslav women taking power away from men in the sphere of familial social networks and asserting their authority ("Žene u bivšoj Jugoslaviji" [Women in former Yugoslavia], 194).

8. *Šljivovica* is a plum brandy (*šljiva* means "plum" in Serbian).

9. Rowlands, "The Role of Memory."

10. Marilyn Strathern argues that relationships in the social world are built not between real entities such as mothers and children but between terms within the code ("The Art of Anthropology," 35)

11. See Milić, "Stari i porodično zbrinjavanje i nega" [Old people and family care], "Transformacija porodice i domaćinstava" [Transformation of family and household], and "The Family and Work"; Blagojević, "Svakodnevica iz ženske perspective" [Everyday life from a female perspective]; Gudac-Dodić, "Položaj žene u Srbiji" [The position of women in Serbia]; and Tomanović, *Sociologija detinjstva* [Sociology of childhood].

12. See Milić, "Stari i porodično zbrinjavanje i nega" [Old people and family care], "Transformacija porodice i domaćinstava" [Transformation of family and household], and "The Family and Work."

13. Tomanović, *Sociologija detinjstva*, 368.

14. Penev, "Demografsko starenje u Srbiji" [Demographic ageing in Serbia]; Milić, "Stari i porodično zbrinjavanje i nega," 446 [Old people and family care].

15. Milosavljević, *Antropologija starosti* [Anthropology of old age], 241.

16. Ibid., 261.

17. Milić, "Stari i porodično zbrinjavanje i nega" [Old people and family care], 462.

18. For comparison with Filipina mothers and their children left behind, see Miller and Madianou, *Migration and the New Media*. For further discussion about normative and processual kinship relationships, see Carsten, *After Kinship*; and Finch and Mason, *Passing On*.

19. See Milić, "Stari i porodično zbrinjavanje i nega" [Old people and family care], "Transformacija porodice i domaćinstava" [Transformation of family and household], and "The Family and Work"; Blagojević, "Svakodnevica iz ženske perspective" [Everyday life from a female perspective]; Gudac-Dodić, "Položaj žene u Srbiji" [The position of women in Serbia].

20. For a fascinating analysis of "cryptomatriarchy" in Serbia and the importance of elderly women, see Simić, "Machismo and Cryptomatriarchy"; see also Simić, "Management of the Male Image"; Burić, "Family, Education and Political Socialization"; and Denich, "Sex and Power," and "Women, Work and Power."

21. Miller, *Dialectics of Shopping*.

22. See, for example, Finch and Mason, *Passing On*; and Carsten, *After Kinship*.

23. Miller, "What Is a Relationship?" See also Miller and Madianou, *Migration and New Media*.

24. Miller, "What Is a Relationship?," 552.

25. In *The Elementary Forms of Religious Life*, Durkheim argues that collective mourning helps restore the social cohesion of the collective after the loss of one or more of its members. Failure to participate in collective mourning is a sign of corrupted group solidarity and social cohesion.

CONCLUSION

W HEN I STARTED TO DESIGN THIS RESEARCH IN 2004, I came across
an anthropologist who specialized in Eastern Europe. Upon hearing
about my project, this expert expressed his doubts about the relevance of
my topic—families in Serbia during the 1990s—and suggested that I instead
study nationalism in Split, Croatia. It was one of my first encounters with
academic dogmatism. This is not to question the proliferation of studies
about nationalism that have dominated the literature about the fall of Yugoslavia but rather to question the absence of research documenting everyday
life during those tragic events.

For millions of people throughout the region of the former Yugoslavia, personal experience was often very different from that portrayed in the
media and from the views of the politicians who claimed to represent them.
Muharem, the family friend and professor from Sarajevo mentioned in the
introduction, could not imagine in May 1991 that the war would spread to
Bosnia. Even more than twenty years later, my informants expressed disbelief about the war in Yugoslavia—none of them saw it coming. None of
them believed that the war could happen in their country and struggled to
accept it even after it had occurred. Moreover, none of them wanted their
sons to fight in that war.

If the fall of the Berlin Wall in 1989 marked the end of socialism in
Eastern Europe, what soon followed in Yugoslavia was not only a change
in the political and economic system but the collapse of one's entire world.
Socialism and Yugoslavia were no more, but there was a horrific, unbeliev-
able war—a conflict in which everyone was forced to take a side. The leaders
of the newly emerged ethnic states would not tolerate ethnic ambivalence
synonymous with Yugoslavia. The foundations of their new ethnic states
had to be laid quickly and firmly. Any doubt about what, why, and how
things happened with Yugoslavia was labeled as a reactionary glorification
of the socialist past at best and as an unpatriotic collaboration with the other
side(s) in the war at worst. The fast-drying mortar on the foundations of the
new ethnic states sealed the ambivalence and disbelief of millions of former
Yugoslavs. If anyone disapproved of the compulsory military draft of men
aged eighteen to sixty-five in Serbia in the 1990s, public discourse drowned

private outcries, labeling conscription evaders as "faggots," "unmanly," and "hiding behind their mothers' skirts."[1] It is no wonder that for years nationalism was considered one of the few topics worth studying in the former Yugoslavia when public discourse allowed for little else to be heard.

As anthropologists, we are privileged to float between private and public spheres. We can document minute, seemingly trivial details from everyday life, including contradictions between words and actions that may escape other social scientists. This focus on intimate, everyday experiences also allows us to capture the personal meaning of public historical events, a context that is often lost to history. Elderly mothers' eagerness to share their experiences, years after their sons and daughters had left the country, testified that what happened in the 1990s was a trauma that they were compelled to voice and validate. This book contains numerous examples of mothers' attempts to mend the rupture in their lives caused by the traumatic departure of their children and concurrent events in their country. Migration's impact on mothers left behind was so profoundly disorienting that they spent years trying to restore a sense of wholeness.

Migration studies are interested in migrants and their experiences but less so in families left behind. However, as we see in this book, those left behind are affected by migration as much as migrants. Mobility and immobility, Noel Salazar and Alan Smart argue, need to be studied alongside one another.[2] But what is mobility? Does it include only physical mobility? When entire social worlds collapse, as we have seen in postcommunist societies, is this immobility or mobility? As I have learned from my London and Belgrade research participants, one can be an alien in one's own country as much as one can feel at home anywhere in the world.

The end of socialism alienated millions of people, ripping away their familiar worlds. Even those who lived in the same apartment building for fifty years experienced changes similar to those associated with migration—where everyday movements and the layout of the familiar world needed to be relearned. One common theme around the region of the former Yugoslavia is a sentiment of displacement—experienced not only by communities that were physically displaced because of the war but especially by people who did not move. The consequences of these tectonic shifts caused by the end of socialism need to be studied, not left to be buried under the foundations of neoliberal ethnic states.

Mothers left behind in 1990s Belgrade reordered their worlds with everyday practices and rituals around the home, making handcrafts, cooking, and writing to their children abroad. Their worlds rapidly shrank in the 1990s as they could not share their pain over the loss of their children, either because of public condemnation or envy. The voices of elderly mothers had no place in public; increasingly, they had no place in a private sphere either, as many of my informants noted there were few friends and family members with whom they could openly talk about their feelings for children they had not seen in years. The lives of mothers left behind turned even more inward into the intimacy of home, where they expressed their emotions in vicarious sacrifices for absent children. Mothers created the presence of their absent children, keeping them alive through actions and everyday rituals that affirmed their relationship.

As long as mothers carried on with family work, sending the odd bottle of homemade spirits or a jar of jam, they affirmed their identity. Feeding the family and thinking about the needs of others is gendered work that constructs women as women. This work in the intimate sphere of the home empowered mothers left behind to persevere when they had lost everything and everyone: their country and stability, social security, middle-class privileges, dignity, and their families. Mothers' work seemed irrational and unnecessary to observers because their migrant children were grown up, could look after themselves, and were financially much better off than their mothers left behind. Despite being aware of all this, mothers persisted with their seemingly irrational work because they were mothers. They felt needed and purposeful in a time and place when few others needed them. In this engagement with the material culture of home, mothers gave meaning to their suffering, objectified in their motherhood.

With the gradual passing of those mothers left behind in the 1990s, there are fewer anchors that keep families connected. These profound changes in family structures and relationships caused by the collapse of socialist Yugoslavia will have lasting consequences. The migrants from the 1990s wave have assimilated in their new countries better than previous generations because of their knowledge, skills, and cosmopolitan outlook.[3] Moreover, while the rule of Slobodan Milošević ended in October 2000, not much progress was made in the relationship between Serbia and this new diaspora. In many ways, the 1990s migrants are lost to Serbia. They are the last Yugoslav generation that refused to participate in its destruction, voting with their feet instead. Their loss to Serbia is thus the loss of a large part of Yugoslav social and cultural heritage. Weiner argues that "the reproduction of kinship is legitimated in each generation through the transmission of inalienable possessions, be they land rights, material objects, or mythic knowledge."[4] Even though this transmission is seemingly conservative, as it calls for the authentication of cosmological origins and kinship, inalienable possessions at the same time are the very symbols of change, "as those in the top ranks of the society may combat change by reconstructing or fabricating genealogies or sacred chronicles in order to identify themselves with the possessions of earlier leaders or dynasties."[5] Without the transmission of inalienable possessions, there is no social reproduction. As we see in this book, the bearers of inalienable possessions at the end of the twentieth century in Serbia were mothers. If their voices remain silenced and their practices are hidden in the intimacy of home, then indeed, inalienable possessions will be lost along with them.

Notes

1. Milićević, "Joining the War."
2. Salazar and Smart, "Introduction."
3. Val Colic-Peisker notes a similar pattern of adaptability among post-1990s Croatian migrants in Australia and the United States (*Migration, Class and Transnational Identities*).
4. Weiner, *Inalienable Possessions*, 10.
5. Ibid., 9.

BIBLIOGRAPHY

Aguirre, Patricia. 2005. *Estrategias de Consumo: qué comen los Argentinos que comen* [Consumption Strategies: what eat the Argentinians who eat]. Buenos Aires: Centro Interdisciplinario para el Estudio de Politicas Publicas.

Alcock, John B., Marko Milivojević, and John J. Horton, eds. 1998. *Conflict in the Former Yugoslavia: An Encyclopedia.* Denver, CO: ABC-Clio.

Antonić, Slobodan. 2002. *Zarobljena zemlja: Srbija za vlade Slobodana Miloševića* [Arrested country: Serbia during the rule of Slobodan Milošević]. Belgrade: Otkrovenje.

Bachelard, Gaston. 1994 [1958]. *The Poetics of Space: The Classic Look at How We Experience Intimate Spaces.* Boston: Beacon Press.

Bajić-Hajduković, Ivana. 2009. "Unmaking Family Relationships: Belgrade Mothers and Their Migrant Children." In *Anthropology and the Individual: A Material Culture Perspective*, edited by D. Miller, 115–30. Oxford, UK: Berg.

———. 2010. "The Lost Matriarch: The Consequences of Remittances on Mother-Child Relationships in Urban Serbia." *Genero—Časopis za feminističku teoriju i studije kulture* 14: 25–48.

———. 2013. "Food, Family, and Memory: Belgrade Mothers and Their Migrant Children." *Food and Foodways: Explorations in the History and Culture of Human Nourishment* 21(1): 46–65.

———. 2014. "Remembering the 'Embargo Cake': The Legacy of Hyperinflation and the UN Sanctions in Serbia." *Contemporary Southeastern Europe—An Interdisciplinary Journal on Southeastern Europe* 1(2): 61–79.

Baker, Catherine. 2015. *The Yugoslav Wars of the 1990s.* London: Palgrave Macmillan.

Bakhtin, Mikhail. 1968. *Rabelais and His World.* Translated by Helene Iswolsky. Cambridge: MIT Press.

Barth, Fredrik. 2002. "An Anthropology of Knowledge." *Current Anthropology* 43(1): 1–18.

Beard, Mary. 2017. *Women and Power: A Manifesto.* London: Profile.

Berger, John. 2013. *Understanding a Photograph.* London: Penguin.

Blagojević, Marina. 1993. "Mladi i roditeljstvo: ka dezideologizaciji roditeljstva" [Youth and parenthood: Towards deideoligization of parenthood]. *Sociologija: časopis za sociologiju, socijalnu psihologiju i socijalnu antropologiju,* 35(3): 327–45.

———. 1994. "War and Everyday Life: Deconstruction of Self-Sacrifice." *Sociologija* 4: 469–82.

———. 1995. "Svakodnevica iz ženske perspektive: samožrtvovanje i beg u privatnost" [Everyday life from a female perspective: Self-sacrifice and finding a refuge in private sphere]. In *Društvene promene i svakodnevni život: Srbija početkom devedesetih* [Social changes and everyday life: Serbia in the early 1990s], edited by S. Bolčić, M. Blagojević, S. Vujović, M. Lazić, A. Milić et al., 181–209. Belgrade: Institut za sociološka istraživanja Filozofskog fakulteta u Beogradu.

———, ed. 1998. *Ka vidljivoj ženskoj istoriji: Ženski pokret u Beogradu 90-ih* [Towards a visible female history: Women's movement in 1990s Belgrade]. Belgrade: Centar za ženske studije, istraživanje i komunikaciju.

———. 2006. "Biti Srbin, biti muško: Rodne politike i etnički identitet u Srbiji devedesetih" [Being Serbian, being a Man: Gender politics and ethnic identity in Serbia of 1990s]. *Časopis za društvenu fenomenologiju i kulturnu dijalogiku, Zeničke sveske* 3: 69–88.

Bock-Luna, Birgit. 2007. *The Past in Exile: Serbian Long-Distance Nationalism and Identity in the Wake of the Third Balkan War.* Berlin: Lit Verlag.

Bogdanović, Marija. 1991. "Materijalni standard društvenih slojeva" [Standard of living of social strata]. In *Srbija krajem osamdesetih: Sociološko istraživanje društvenih nejednakosti i neusklađenosti* [Serbia in the late 1980s: Sociological research of inequality and discrepancies], edited by Popović, M., M. Bogdanović, R. Petrović, M. Blagojević, A. Milić, V. Grbić, S. Bolčić et al. 241–73. Belgrade: Institut za sociološka istraživanja Filozofskog fakulteta u Beogradu.

Bogićević, Biljana, Gorana Krstić, and Boško Mijatović. 2002. *Siromaštvo u Srbiji i reforma državne pomoći siromašnima* [Poverty in Serbia and a reform of the state help for the poor]. Belgrade: Centar za Liberalno-demokratske studije.

Bourdieu, Pierre. 1977. *Outline of a Theory of Practice.* Cambridge: Cambridge University Press.

———. 1986. "The Forms of Capital." In *Handbook of Theory and Research for the Sociology of Education*, edited by J. G. Richardson, 241–58. Westport, CT: Greenwood.

———. 1990. *The Logic of Practice.* Stanford, CA: Stanford University Press.

Božinović, Neda. 1998. "Žene u modernizacijskim procesima u Jugoslaviji i Srbiji" [Women in modernization processes in Yugoslavia and Serbia]. In *Srbija u modernizacijskim procesima 19. i 20. veka.* Knjiga 2, *Položaj žene kao merilo modernizacije: naučni skup* [Serbia in modernization processes in the 19th and 20th centuries. Book 2, The position of woman as a measure of modernization: Scientific conference], edited by L. Perović, M. Milenković, B. Prpa-Jovanović, and D. Stojanović, 505–33. Belgrade: Institut za noviju istoriju Srbije.

Brown, Keith. 2001. "Beyond Ethnicity: The Politics of Urban Nostalgia in Modern Macedonia." *Journal of Mediterranean Studies* 11(2): 417–42.

Burguière, André. 2004. "Le concept d'autocontrainte et son usage historique." In *Norbert Elias et l'anthropologie*, edited by S. Chevalier and J.-M. Privat, 71–81. Paris: CNRS Editions.

Burić, Olivera. 1972. "Family, Education and Political Socialization of Youth in Yugoslavia." *International Journal of Sociology of the Family* 2(1): 21–29.

Burić, Olivera, Vesna Pešić, Anđelka Milić, Milosav Milosavljević, Sreten Vujović, and Miloš Nemanjić. 1980. *Porodica i društveni sistem: sociološko-politikološko istraživanje o povezanosti porodice i institucija socijalističkog samoupravnog društvenog sistema Jugoslavije* [Family and a social system: socio-political research about relatedness of family and institutions in the socialist self-managing Yugoslav social system]. Belgrade: Institut za socijalnu politiku.

Butler, Judith. 1999. *Gender Trouble: Feminism and the Subversion of Identity.* New York: Routledge.

Caldwell, Melissa. 2004. *Not by Bread Alone: Social Support in the New Russia.* Berkeley: University of California Press.

Carsten, Janet. 2004. *After Kinship.* Cambridge: Cambridge University Press.

Čerčil, Vinston [Churchill, Winston]. 1964. *Drugi svetski rat. Tom 1, Bura se sprema* [The second world war. Vol. 1, The gathering storm]. Translated by Milica Mihailović. Belgrade: Prosveta.

Clifford, James. 2001. "The Last Discussant," in *Irony in Action: Anthropology, Practice, and the Moral Imagination*, edited by J.W. Fernandez and M. Taylor Huber, 253–59, Chicago and London: University of Chicago Press.

Cohen, Lenard J., and Jasna Dragović-Soso. 2008. *State Collapse in South-Eastern Europe: New Perspectives on Yugoslavia's Disintegration*. West Lafayette, IN: Purdue University Press.

Colic-Peisker, Val. 2008. *Migration, Class and Transnational Identities: Croatians in Australia and America*. Chicago: University of Illinois Press.

Čolović, Ivan. 2002. *The Politics of Symbol in Serbia: Essays in Political Anthropology*. London: Hurst.

Ćopić, Branko. 1964. "Odgovor zemljaku" [A Reply to a Compatriot]. In *Pjesme* [Poems], 53–54. Belgrade: Prosveta/Svjetlost.

Counihan, Carole. 1999. *The Anthropology of Food and Body: Gender, Meaning and Power*. New York: Routledge.

———. 2002. "Food as Woman's Voice in San Luis Valley of Colorado." In *Food in the USA*, edited by C. Counihan, 295–304. New York: Routledge.

———. 2004. *Around the Tuscan Table: Food, Family, and Gender in Twentieth-Century Florence*. London: Routledge.

Delević, Milica. 1998. "Economic Sanctions as a Foreign Policy Tool: The Case of Yugoslavia." *International Journal of Peace Studies* 3(1). http://www.gmu.edu/programs/icar/ijps /vol3_1/Delvic.htm.

Denich, Bette. 1974. "Sex and Power in the Balkans." In *Woman, Culture and Society*, edited by M. Z. Rosaldo and L. Lamphere, 243–63. Stanford, CA: Stanford University Press.

———. 1976. "Urbanization and Women's Role in Yugoslavia." *Anthropological Quarterly* 49(1): 11–19.

———. 1977. "Women, Work and Power in Modern Yugoslavia." In *Sexual Stratification: A Cross-Cultural View*, edited by A. Schlegel, 215–44. New York: Columbia University Press.

DeVault, Marjorie. 1991. *Feeding the Family: The Social Organization of Caring as Gendered Work*. Chicago: University of Chicago Press.

Dević, Ana. 2016. "What Nationalism Has Buried: Yugoslav Social Scientists on the Crisis, Grassroots Powerlessness and Yugoslavia." In *Social Inequalities and Discontent in Yugoslav Socialism*, edited by R. Archer, I. Duda, and P. Stubbs, 21–37. London: Routledge.

Dinkić, Mlađan. 1996. *Ekonomija destrukcije: velika pljačka naroda* [The economy of destruction: A big robbery of the nation]. Belgrade: Stubovi kulture.

Douglas, Mary. 1966. *Purity and Danger: An Analysis of Concepts of Pollution and Taboo*. London: Routledge.

Durkheim, Émile. [1915] 1971. *The Elementary Forms of Religious Life*. London: Allen and Unwin.

Duruz, Jean. 1999. "Food as Nostalgia: Eating the Fifties and Sixties." *Australian Historical Studies* 113: 231–50.

Edwards, Elizabeth. 1999. "Photographs as Objects of Memory." In *Material Memories: Design and Evocation*, edited by M. Kwint, C. Breward, and J. Aynsley, 221–36. Oxford, UK: Berg.

Eyal, Gil, Iván Szelényi, and Eleanor R. Townsley. 1998. *Making Capitalism without Capitalists: Class Formation and Elite Struggling in Post-Communist Central Europe*. London: Verso.

Fabian, Johannes. 1983. *Time and the Other: How Anthropology Makes Its Object*. New York: Columbia University Press.

Finch, Janet, and Jennifer Mason. 2000. *Passing On: Kinship and Inheritance in England*. London: Routledge.

Gagnon, V. P. Jr. 2004. *The Myth of Ethnic War: Serbia and Croatia in the 1990s*. Ithaca, NY: Cornell University Press.

Geertz, Clifford. 1963. *Agricultural Involution: The Process of Ecological Change in Indonesia*. Berkeley: University of California Press.

Gell, Alfred. 1999. *The Art of Anthropology: Essays and Diagrams*. London: Athlone.

Glenny, Misha. 2000. *The Balkans: Nationalism, War and the Great Powers, 1804–1999*. New York: Viking.

Gow, James, and Cathie Carmichael. 1999. *Slovenia and the Slovenes*. London: C. Hurst.

Gudac-Dodić, Vera. 2006. "Položaj žene u Srbiji (1945–2000)" [The position of women in Serbia, 1945–2000]. In *Žene i deca: Srbija u modernizacijskim procesima XIX i XX veka. Knjiga 4* [Women and children: Serbia in modernization processes in the 19th and 20th centuries. Book 4], edited by L. Perović, 33–130. Belgrade: Helsinški odbor za ljudska prava u Srbiji.

Guidonet Riera, Alicia. 2011. "The Spanish Civil War and Its Aftermath: Eating Strategies and Social Change." In *Food and War in Twentieth Century Europe*, edited by I. Zweininger-Bargielowska, R. Duffett, and A. Drouard, 99–110. Farnham, UK: Ashgate.

Halbwachs, Maurice. [1925] 1980. *Collective Memory*. New York: Harper and Row.

Hallam, Elizabeth, and Jenny Hockey. 2001. *Death, Memory and Material Culture*. Oxford, UK: Berg.

Hanke, Steve H., and Nicholas Krus. 2012. "World Hyperinflations." Cato Working Paper No. 8, August 15. Institute for Applied Economics, Global Health, and the Study of Business Enterprise, John Hopkins University, Baltimore, MD. https://object.cato.org/sites/cato.org/files/pubs/pdf/workingpaper-8_1.pdf.

Herzfeld, Michael. 2001. "Irony and Power: Toward a Politics of Mockery in Greece." In *Irony in Action: Anthropology, Practice and the Moral Imagination*, edited by J. W. Fernandez and M. Taylor Huber, 63–83. Chicago: University of Chicago Press.

Hinde, Natasha. 2015. "Vegetable Oil Linked to Cancer and Dementia, Experts Recommend Butter, Lard and Olive Oil Instead." *Huffington Post UK*, November 9. https://www.huffingtonpost.co.uk/2015/11/09/cooking-with-vegetable-oil-associated-with-cancer_n_8509382.html.

Holtzman, Jon D. 2006. "Food and Memory." *Annual Review of Anthropology* 35: 361–78.

Horvat, Branko. 1969. *Ogled o jugoslavenskom društvu* [An essay about Yugoslav society], Zagreb: Mladost.

Hughes, Donna M., Lepa Mlađenović, and Zorica Mršević. 1995. "Feminist Resistance in Serbia." *European Journal of Women's Studies* 2(4): 509–32.

Humphrey, Caroline. 1995. "Creating a Culture of Disillusionment: Consumption in Moscow, a Chronicle of Changing Times." In *Worlds Apart: Modernity through the Prism of the Local*, edited by D. Miller, 43–69. Oxford, UK: Berg.

Humphrey, Caroline, and Ruth Mandel, eds. 2002. *Market and Moralities: Ethnographies of Postsocialism*. Oxford, UK: Berg.

Isić, Momčilo. 2006. "Dete i žena na selu u Srbiji između dva svetska rata" [Child and woman in Serbian village between the two world wars]. In *Žene i deca: Srbija u modernizacijskim procesima XIX i XX veka. Knjiga 4* [Women and children: Serbia in modernization processes in the 19th and 20th centuries, book 4], edited by L. Perović, 131–59. Belgrade: Helsinški odbor za ljudska prava u Srbiji.

Jansen, Stef. 2005a. *Antinacionalizam: etnografija otpora u Beogradu i Zagrebu*. Belgrade: Dvadeseti vek.

———. 2005b. "Who's Afraid of White Socks? Towards a Critical Understanding of Post-Yugoslav Urban Self-Perceptions." *Ethnologia Balkanica* 9: 151–67.

Jelavich, Barbara. 1983. *History of the Balkans*. Cambridge: Cambridge University Press.

Jones, Toni. 2012. "The Great British Bake Graph! Trend Timeline Reveals How Our Love of Home Baking Has Risen and Flopped Each Decade Since the 1900s (and We Are Now Baking More Than Ever)." *Daily Mail*, October 16. https://www.dailymail.co.uk/femail /article-2218486/The-Great-British-Bake-Graph-Trend-timeline-reveals-love-home -baking-risen-flopped-decade-1900s-baking-EVER.html.

Jugoslovenska, Narodna Armija. 1983. *Uputstvo o pripremanju jela u JNA u ratu* [A manual for food preparation in the Yugoslav People's Army at war]. Belgrade: Vojnoizdavački Zavod.

Kaser, Karl. 1995. *Familie und Verwandtschaft auf dem Balkan. Analyse einder untergehenden Kultur*. Vienna-Cologne-Weimar: Böhlau.

———. 2008. *Patriarchy after Patriarchy: Gender Relations in Turkey and in the Balkans, 1500–2000*. Munster: Lit Verlag.

King, Russell, and Julie Vullnetari. 2006. "Orphan Pensioners and Migrating Grandparents: The Impact of Mass Migration on Older People in Rural Albania." *Ageing and Society* 26: 783–816.

Komarovsky, Mary. [1940] 2004. *The Unemployed Man and His Family*. New York: Altamira.

Kopytoff, Igor. 2004. "Commoditizing Kinship in America." In *Consuming Motherhood*, edited by. J. Taylor, L. Layne, and D. Wozniak, 271–73. New Brunswick, NJ: Rutgers University Press.

Kovačević, Miladin, Kristina Pavlović, and Vladimir Šutić. 2015. *Upotreba informaciono-komunikacionih tehnologija u Republici Srbiji* [The use of information and communication technologies in the Republic of Serbia]. Belgrade: Republički Zavod za Statistiku Srbije.

Krivokapić, B. 2007. "Dijaspora pomaže, ali nema investicija" [Diaspora helps, but there are no investments]. *Blic*, September 15. https://www.blic.rs/biznis/dijaspora-pomaze-ali -nema-investicija/336ksqq.

Lee, Sandra Soo-Jin. 2000. "Dys-appearing Tongues and Bodily Memories: The Aging of First-Generation Resident Koreans in Japan." *Ethos* 28(2): 198–223.

Mankekar, Purnima. 2002. "'India Shopping': Indian Grocery Stores and Transnational Configuration of Belonging." *Ethnos* 67(1): 75–98.

Matić, Miloš. 2005. "Urban Economies in a Rural Manner: Family Economizing in Socialist Serbian Center." *Ethnologia Balkanica* 9: 131–49.

Mauss, Marcel. [1956] 2002. *The Gift: The Form and Reason for Exchange in Archaic Societies*. London: Routledge.

Mesure, Susie. 2013. "Feeling Kneady: The Rise of Artisan Baking." *Independent* (UK), October 6. https://www.independent.co.uk/life-style/food-and-drink/news/feeling -kneady-the-rise-of-artisan-baking-8861304.html.

Mikavica, Aleksandar. 2006. "Dosta šalju—malo ulažu" [They send a lot—invest a little] *Politika*, July 10. http://www.politika.rs/scc/clanak/12204.

Milić, Anđelka. 1991. "Socijalna mreža porodičnih odnosa i društveni slojevi" [Social Strata and Social Networks of Family Relation]. In *Srbija krajem osamdesetih*.

Sociološko istraživanje društvenih nejednakosti i neusklađenosti [Serbia in the late 1980s: Sociological research of inequality and discrepancies], edited by Popović, M., M. Bogdanović, R. Petrović, M. Blagojević, A. Milić, V. Grbić, S. Bolčić et al., 111–46. Belgrade: Institut za sociološka istraživanja Filozofskog fakulteta u Beogradu.

———. 1998. "Stari ljudi u procesu društvene tranzicije" [The elderly in the process of social transition], *Socijalna misao*, 5(2): 29–40.

———. 2004a. "Stari i porodično zbrinjavanje i nega" [Old people and family care]. In *Društvena transformacija i strategije društvenih grupa: svakodnevica Srbije na početku trećeg milenijuma* [Social transformation and strategies of social groups: Everyday life of Serbia at the beginning of the millennium], edited by A. Milić, 443–63. Belgrade: Institut za sociološka istraživanja Filozofskog fakulteta u Beogradu.

———. 2004b. "Transformacija porodice i domaćinstava—zastoj i strategije preživljavanja" [Transformation of the Family and Households: Stagnation and Survival Strategies]. In *Društvena transformacija i strategije društvenih grupa: svakodnevica Srbije na početku trećeg milenijuma* [Social transformation and strategies of social groups: Everyday life of Serbia at the Beginning of the Millenium], edited by A. Milić, 315–45. Belgrade: Institut za sociološka istraživanja Filozofskog fakulteta u Beogradu.

———. 2008. "Žene u bivšoj Jugoslaviji: Drugačiji pogled na učinke socijalizma u promeni društvenog položaja žena" [Women in former Yugoslavia: A different view on the effects of socialism in the change of social position of women in ex-Yugoslavia]. In *Društvo rizika: Promene, nejednakosti i socijalni problemi u današnjoj Srbiji* [Risk society: Changes, inequalities and social issues in today's Serbia], edited by S. Vujović, 181–98. Belgrade: Institut za sociološka istraživanja Filozofskog fakulteta u Beogradu.

Milić, Anđelka. 2007. "The Family and Work in the Post-Socialist Transition of Serbia: 1991–2006." *International Review of Sociology*, 17(2): 359–80.

Milić, Anđelka, ed. 2004. *Društvena transformacija i strategije društvenih grupa: svakodnevica Srbije na početku trećeg milenijuma* [Social transformation and strategies of social groups: Everyday life of Serbia at the beginning of the millennium]. Belgrade: Institut za sociološka istraživanja Filozofskog fakulteta u Beogradu.

Milićević, Aleksandra Sasha. 2006. "Joining the War: Masculinity, Nationalism and War Participation in the Balkans War of Succession, 1991–1995." *Nationalities Papers* 34(3): 265–87.

Miller, Daniel. 2001. *The Dialectics of Shopping*. Chicago: University of Chicago Press.

———. 2007. "What Is a Relationship? Is Kinship Negotiated Experience?," *Ethnos* 72(4): 535–54.

Miller, Daniel, and Mirca Madianou. 2011. *Migration and New Media: Transnational Families and Polymedia*. New York: Routledge.

Milosavljević, Ljubica. 2014. *Antropologija starosti: Domovi (Konstruisanje starosti kao društvenog problema kroz organizovano domsko zbrinjavanje—od sirotinjskih do staračkih domova)* [Anthropology of old age: Nursing homes (a construction of ageing as a social problem through organized care—from pauper homes to nursing homes)]. Belgrade: Filozofski Fakultet Univerziteta u Beogradu.

Mosley, Michael. 2015. "Why It's Healthier to Cook with Lard Than Sunflower Oil: Extraordinary Experiment Shows Everything We've Been Told about Cooking Oils Is Wrong." *Daily Mail*, July 28. https://www.dailymail.co.uk/health/article-3176558 /It-s-healthier-cook-LARD-sunflower-oil-Extraordinary-experiment-shows-ve-told -cooking-oils-wrong.html.

Moss, Rachel. 2015. "Lard May Be Healthier Than Sunflower Oil for Cooking, BBC Show 'Trust Me I'm A Doctor' Reveals." *Huffington Post UK*, July 28. https://www .huffingtonpost.co.uk/2015/07/28/bbc-trust-me-im-a-doctor-lard-healthier-sunflower -oil_n_7885196.html.

Munn, Nancy D. 1986. *The Fame of Gawa: A Symbolic Study of Value Transformation in a Massim (Papua New Guinea) Society*. Cambridge: Cambridge University Press.

Naji, Myriem. 2009. "Gender and Materiality in-the-Making: The Manufacture of Sirwan Femininities through Weaving in Southern Morocco." *Journal of Material Culture* 14(1): 47–73.

Newman, Katherine. 1988. *Falling from Grace: The Experience of Downward Mobility in the American Middle Class*. New York: Free Press.

Palmberger, Monika, and Jelena Tošić. 2016. "Introduction: Memories on the Move— Experiencing Mobility, Rethinking the Past." In *Memories on the Move: Experiencing Mobility, Rethinking the Past*, edited by M. Palmberger and J. Tošić, 1–16. London: Palgrave Macmillan.

Pamuk, Orhan. 2006. *Istanbul: Memories and the City*. London: Faber and Faber.

Papić, Žarana. 1999. "Women in Serbia: Post-Communism, War and Nationalist Mutations." In *Gender Politics in the Western Balkans: Women and Society in Yugoslavia and the Yugoslav Successor States*, edited by S. P. Ramet, 153–69. University Park: Penn State University Press.

Parreñas, Rhacel S. 2005. *Children of Global Migration: Transnational Families and Gendered Woes*. Stanford, CA: Stanford University Press.

Patico, Jennifer. 2008. *Consumption and Social Change in a Post-Soviet Middle Class*. Stanford, CA: Stanford University Press.

Patterson, Patrick H. 2011. *Bought and Sold: Living and Losing the Good Life in Socialist Yugoslavia*. Ithaca, NY: Cornell University Press.

Pavličić, Pavao. 2018. *Kruh i mast—Šapudl* [Bread and lard]. Zagreb: Mozaik knjiga.

Pekić, Borislav. 1987. *Godine koje su pojeli skakavci: uspomene iz zatvora ili Antropopeja 1948–1954* [The years the locusts have devoured: memories from prison or anthropoeia 1948–1954]. Belgrade: BIGZ.

Penev, Goran. 2002. "Demografsko starenje u Srbiji" [Demographic ageing in Serbia]. *Demografski pregled* 11(3): 1–3.

Perianu, Catherina. 2008. "Précarité Alimentaire, Austérité: Manger pendant la dernière décennie communiste en Roumanie" [Food insecurity and austerity: Eating in the last decade of communism in Romania]. *Anthropology of Food* (online) 6 (September). http://journals.openedition.org/aof/4513.

Perović, Latinka. 2006. *Izmedju anarhije i autokratije: srpsko društvo na prelazima vekova (XIX–XXI)* [Between anarchy and autocracy: Serbian society in-between the centuries (XIX–XXI)]. Belgrade: Helsinški odbor za ljudska prava.

Petree, Jennifer, and Nilim Baruah. 2006. *A Study of Migrant-Sending Households in Serbia-Montenegro Receiving Remittances from Switzerland*. Geneva: International Organization for Migration.

Petridou, Elia. 2001. "The Taste of Home." In *Home Possessions*, edited by D. Miller, 87–104. London: Berg.

Popović, Mihailo V., M. Bogdanović, S. Vujović, B. Džuverović, J. Petrović, M. Davidović, D. Mrkšić, et al. 1987. *Društvene nejednakosti* [Social inequalities]. Belgrade: Institut za sociološka istraživanja Filozofskog fakulteta.

Proust, Marcel. 1992. *In Search of Lost Time. Volume 1, Swann's Way.* Translated by C. K. Scott Moncrieff and T. Kilmartin. London: Chatto and Windus.

Radulović, Jelena. 1942. *Ratni kuvar: Zbirka od preko 200 recepata o spravljanju jela bez mesa i uz najveću štednju namirnica čija je potrošnja racionirana* [War cookbook: A collection of over 200 recipes about cooking without meat and most frugally using the rationed ingredients]. Belgrade: n.p.

Ramet, Sabrina P. 2005. *The Three Yugoslavias: State-Building and Legitimation, 1918–2005.* Bloomington: Indiana University Press.

Ray, Krishnendu. 2004. *The Migrant's Table: Meals and Memories in Bengali-American Households.* Philadelphia: Temple University Press.

Republički zavod za statistiku Srbije. 2005. *Žene i muškarci u Srbiji* [Women and men in Serbia]. Translated by T. Ćosović. Belgrade: Publikum.

Rihtman-Auguštin, Dunja. 2000. *Ulice moga grada* [The streets in my town]. Belgrade: Biblioteka XX Vek.

Roden, Claudia. 1974. *Book of Middle Eastern Food.* New York: Vintage.

Roux, Michel. 2011. "Great British Food Revival: The Lost Art of Bread-Making." *BBC Food Blog*, March 9. https://www.bbc.co.uk/blogs/food/2011/03/great-british-revival-the-lost .shtml.

Rowlands, Michael. 1993. "The Role of Memory in the Transmission of Culture." *World Archaeology* 25(2): 141–51.

Roy, Parama. 2002. "Reading Communities and Culinary Communities: The Gastropoetics of the South Asian Diaspora." *Positions* 10(2): 471–502.

Sahlins, Marshall. 1972. *Stone Age Economics.* New York: de Gruyter.

Salazar, Noel B., and Alan Smart. 2011. "Introduction: Anthropological Takes on (Im) Mobility." *Identities: Global Studies in Culture and Power* 18: i–ix.

Seremetakis, C. Nadia. 1994. "The Memory of the Senses. Part I: Marks of the Transitory." In *The Senses Still: Perception and Memory as Material Culture in Modernity*, edited by C. Nadia Seremetakis, 1–19. Boulder, CO: Westview.

———, ed. 1994. *The Senses Still: Perception and Memory as Material Culture in Modernity.* Boulder, CO: Westview.

Silber, Laura, and Alan Little. 1997. *Yugoslavia: Death of a Nation.* London: Penguin.

Simić, Andrei. 1969. "Management of the Male Image in Yugoslavia." *Anthropological Quarterly* 42(2): 89–101.

———. 1973. *The Peasant Urbanites: A Study of Rural-Urban Mobility in Serbia.* New York: Seminar.

———. 1983. "Machismo and Cryptomatriarchy: Power, Affect, and Authority in the Contemporary Yugoslav Family." *Ethnos* 11(1–2): 66–86.

Slapšak, Svetlana. 2016. *Ravnoteža* [Equilibrium]. Belgrade: Laguna.

Šljukić, Srđan, and Marica Šljukić. 2012. *Zemlja i ljudi—seljaštvo i društvena struktura* [The land and the people—peasantry and social structure]. Novi Sad: Mediterran.

Spasić, Ivana. 2006. "ASFALT: The Construction of Urbanity in Everyday Discourse in Serbia." *Ethnologia Balkanica* 10: 211–27.

Stamenković, Stojan, and Aleksandra Pošarac, eds. 1994. *Makroekonomska stabilizacija: Alternativni pristup* [Macroeconomic stabilization: An alternative approach]. Belgrade: Institut ekonomskih nauka.

Stanković, Vladimir. 2014. *Popis stanovništva, domaćinstva i stanova 2011. u Republici Srbiji: Srbija u procesu spoljnih migracija* [Census of population and households 2011 in the

Republic of Serbia: Serbia in the process of emigration]. Belgrade: Republički Zavod za Statistiku.

Stevens, Carolyn. 1997. *On the Margins of Japanese Society: Volunteers and the Welfare of the Urban Underclass*. London: Routledge.

Sutton, David. 2001. *Remembrance of Repasts: Anthropology of Food and Memory*. Oxford, UK: Berg.

Thring, Oliver. 2011. "Consider Lard." Word of Mouth Blog, *The Guardian*, February 15. https://www.theguardian.com/lifeandstyle/wordofmouth/2011/feb/15/consider-lard.

Todorović, Tomislav. 1993. "Dnevno umire desetak bolesnika" [Ten patients die daily]. *Politika*, November 17, p. 1.

Tomanović, Smiljka. 2004. *Sociologija detinjstva: sociološka hrestomatija* [Sociology of childhood: Sociological chrestomathy]. Belgrade: Zavod za udžbenike i nastavna sredstva.

Verdery, Katherine. 1999. *The Political Lives of Dead Bodies: Reburial and Postsocialist Change*. New York: Columbia University Press.

Vujović, Sreten. 1997. *Grad u senci rata—ogledi o gradu, siromastvu i sukobima* [A city in the shadow of a war—views about the city, poverty and conflicts]. Novi Sad: Prometej and Institut za Sociologiju Filozofskog fakulteta u Beogradu.

Warnier, Jean-Pierre. 2001. "A Praxeological Approach to Subjectivation in a Material World." *Journal of Material Culture* 6(1): 5–24.

———. 2006. "Inside and Outside: Surfaces and Containers." In *Handbook of Material Culture*, edited by C. Tilley, W. Keane, S. Küchler, M. Rowlands, and P. Spyer, 186–96. London: Sage.

Weiner, Annette B. 1992. *Inalienable Possessions: The Paradox of Keeping-While-Giving*. Berkeley: University of California Press.

Wilde, Alan. 1981. *Horizons of Assent: Modernism, Postmodernism, and the Ironic Imagination*. Baltimore: Johns Hopkins University Press.

Zakon o amnestiji [The amnesty law]. 2006. *Beograd: Službeni Glasnik Republike Srbije*, no. 33/06.

Zelizer, Viviana A. 1994. *Pricing the Priceless Child: The Changing Social Value of Children*. Princeton, NJ: Princeton University Press.

INDEX

IVANA BAJIĆ-HAJDUKOVIĆ is Adjunct Professor of Food Studies
at Syracuse University in London, United Kingdom.

www.ingramcontent.com/pod-product-compliance
Lightning Source LLC
Chambersburg PA
CBHW031438280326
41927CB00038B/952